Heavenly Weekends

CITY *and* COMPANY • NEW YORK

Heavenly Weekends

TRAVEL *without a* CAR

----

52 DAYTRIPS,

OVERNIGHT, *and*

WEEKEND GETAWAYS

near NEW YORK

SUSAN CLEMETT *&*

GENA VANDESTIENNE

With illustrations by Molly O'Gorman

Library of Congress Cataloging-in-Publication Data
is available upon request.

ISBN 1-885492-59-6

First Edition

Printed in the United States of America

City & Company

22 West 23rd Street

New York, NY 10010

Publisher's Note: Neither City & Company nor the author has any interest, financial or personal, in the locations listed in this book. No fees were paid or services rendered in exchange for inclusion in these pages. While every effort was made to ensure accuracy at the time of publication, please call ahead to confirm details.

Table of Contents

Introduction   *10*

One Hour *or* Less

CONNECTICUT

NEW JERSEY

Two *and a* Half Hours

Introduction

WE ARE TWO WOMEN who live and work in Manhattan and have a passion for exploring the towns, villages, and cities surrounding New York City during the weekends. Our weekend voyages have brought a tremendous sense of joy and liberation to our lives, and have provided us with the physical and emotional resilience to return to New York and cope with its hectic pace. Traveling without a car, we have personally visited every town and stayed at every hotel, inn, and bed and breakfast we feature.

We enjoyed our adventures so much that we created this book to share our experiences with you, so that you too can take advantage of New York's proximity to such a spectacular array of amazing getaways. Whether you're a couple, just friends, a family, mother and daughter, father and son, or single, you'll find a wide variety of destinations in this book to tickle your fancy.

Since, like many New Yorkers, neither of us owns a car, we have targeted destinations that are easily accessible by public transportation and offer lodging facilities within close proximity of the train or bus station. Furthermore, many hotels will send a courtesy van to pick you up and return you to the station, otherwise taxis are always an option and are usually fairly economical.

Get on the bus

One advantage we discovered of traveling by bus is that it provides the opportunity to see what life is like on the main streets of towns and villages. It is also a great way to take in the exquisite scenery of the region. And you might be pleasantly surprised to hear that most buses we traveled on were extremely comfortable—with reclining seats, overhead reading lights, and air vents. By the way, if you haven't paid a recent visit to the much-maligned Port Authority bus station, it's been entirely renovated and bears no resemblance to its former self. The terminal now has several pleasant eateries, a wide range of shops and vendors, and *no* panhandling is permitted. Soothing chamber music plays on the P.A. system and can help relax the tensest of travelers.

Off-season is _in-season_

We recommend off-season stays for the most popular seasonal resort areas because in-season stays require advance planning and a willingness to put up with crowds—and of course are much more costly. For example, for only $50 a night during the fall you can stay in a spacious guesthouse in Sag Harbor. The temperature might be a little chillier than during the summer, but your woodburning fireplace and canopy bed will certainly warm your spirits.

The extended weekend

A good way to extend your overnight stay is to arrive at your destination early on Saturday morning (even if your room is not ready and check-in time isn't until 2 P.M.). You can drop off your bags and begin your weekend adventures as soon as you arrive. When you check in, request a late checkout for the following day. This assures you of a relaxing morning that you can spend at the pool, having a leisurely breakfast, or just indulging in a Sunday morning sleep-in without having to pack your belongings before the hotel maid arrives at 11 A.M. And most hotels and inns are glad to hold your bags for the afternoon so you can continue to explore the town and use the facilities until it's time to return to the city on Sunday evening.

Explore

We offer our restaurant recommendations for each destination and provide telephone numbers when advance reservations are necessary, but we encourage you to explore and discover your own favorites. After all, what fun is travel without a little sense of adventure?

More information

If you'd like more information about a town you want to visit, call the Chamber of Commerce or historical society (we provide many of these telephone numbers in the text), or inquire at the hotel or inn where you plan to stay. You may also be able to track down some useful information on the World Wide Web.

Useful Transportation Numbers

TRAINS:

Amtrak	800-872-7245
	212-630-6400
Long Island Railroad	718-217-5477
Metro North	212-532-4900

BUSES:

Port Authority Bus Terminal	212-564-8484
Academy	212-964-6600
Adirondack Trailways	800-858-8555
Bonanza	800-556-3815
DeCamp	973-783-7500
Greyhound	800-231-2222
Hampton Jitneys	800-936-0440
Lakeland	973-366 0600
New Jersey Transit	973-762-5100
Omega Charter	800-944-1001
Peter Pan Trailways	800-343-9999
Red & Tan Lines	800-772-3689
Short Line	800-631-8405
Suburban Lines	800-262-2497
Transbridge	800-962-9135

One Hour

or

Less

Greenwich, CT

... mansions, millionaires, and the Bruce Museum.

DAY OR WEEKEND TRIP; KID-FRIENDLY

Getting There

Metro-North trains (212-532-4900) leave Grand Central Station for Greenwich, Connecticut, throughout the day. When you get off the train, walk down the hill to the busiest street in town—Greenwich Avenue.

Being There: Then and Now

In the mid-1800s when the railroad came to town, Greenwich developed as a resort area catering to New Yorkers who lived less than an hour away by train. Gracious hotels and estates were built by Gimbel, Havemeyer, and Rockefeller along the shore of Long Island Sound.

Today it's a high income bedroom community with large homes, beautiful shops, and elegant restaurants. Little parks provide resting spots, and there's a small-town atmosphere that attracts shoppers from neighboring towns.

Seeing and Doing

The Bruce Museum (One Museum Drive, 203-869-0376) was once the residence of Robert Bruce, a successful textile manufacturer. In 1908, he bequeathed his Victorian stone mansion on a hill overlooking the harbor to the town, with the understanding that it would be turned into a public museum of history and art. The Bruce Museum became so popular that a large and stunning new facility opened its doors in 1933.

The Bruce Museum is a short walk from the train station. When you leave the station, turn left and walk along Steamboat Road until you come to Museum Drive, on your left. Walk up the hill to the museum. This is a perfect place to take children of all ages. The little ones will enjoy the big outdoor playground.

The Bruce boasts a sizable collection of American Impressionist art and an environmental science exhibit that includes a woodland diorama recreating early spring 500 years ago along the Sound. The Marine Room features living specimens from the Long Island Sound in a large touch tank—visitors are permitted to hold, stroke, and handle the sea creatures within.

The four-screen Plaza Theater, right next to the railroad trestle at the corner of Greenwich and Railroad Streets, specializes in independent and foreign films.

Eating There

Greenwich Avenue, a very cosmopolitan boulevard, is crammed with bistros, cafes, and elegant restaurants featuring cuisines of many countries. Maneros (559 Steamboat Road, 203-869-0049) is a sprawling, simply furnished, and popular family steak house. Greenwich Harbor Inn (500 Steamboat Road, 203-661-9800), the hotel we recommend for an overnight stay, has two charming eateries: Pier 92 Pub is great for a casual meal and drinks, either inside or on the patio overlooking the water. Atlantis Restaurant serves superb seafood prepared by world-class chefs.

Staying There

The Greenwich Harbor Inn, located alongside busy Greenwich Harbor, where yachts and pleasure boats are moored, has a lovely ambiance. Guest rooms are decorated in soft colonial colors and furnished with eighteenth-century English reproductions. Many rooms have private balconies overlooking the harbor and offshore Connecticut islands. Room rates are affordable.

To reach the Greenwich Harbor Inn, turn left as you leave the train station and walk under the railroad trestle. The inn is on your right, about two blocks away.

Old Greenwich, Ct.

. . . New England charm; Hyatt luxury

DAY OR WEEKEND TRIP

Getting There

It's a 45-minute trip by the Metro-North train (212-532-4900) from Grand Central Station. If you're planning to spend the night at the Hyatt Regency Hotel (203-637-1234), call from the station and they'll send a van or taxi to pick you up for the three-minute ride up the hill.

Being There: Then and Now

A wonderful fall or midwinter weekend combines the luxury of the Greenwich Hyatt Regency with the quaint village of Old Greenwich. Explore the village before you go to the hotel, or relax at the Hyatt for a while and then hike down the hill into town.

The architectural style of many of the homes and storefronts of Old Greenwich is in keeping with the town's seventeenth-century beginnings. Simple whitewashed brick and clapboard buildings perch on either side of Sound Beach Avenue, the tree-lined main street. Graceful wooden benches and barrels of flowering plants outside the shops encourage you to just sit awhile and enjoy this charming hamlet.

Seeing and Doing

To explore Old Greenwich from the train station, turn right and walk down the sloping road to Sound Beach Avenue. Turn right again to find the pretty shops along this main street. Turn left and walk toward the First Congregational Church, established in 1665, and the adjoining hilly cemetery with tombstones dating back to the seventeenth century. Across from the church is the picturesque village park, an oasis of tiny stone bridges, meandering streams, wide expanses of lawn, and a glistening lake. Binney, of Binney and Smith, makers of Crayola crayons, donated this park to the village in 1928.

Across the road from the park is the Parrot Memorial Library, built in 1931. The building is reminiscent of the Jefferson Memorial in Washington, D.C. Inside, clusters of wingback chairs provide a homey setting to relax.

Eating There

The Hyatt has two restaurants: Winfields Cafe, where you can dine on casual fare in the gardenlike atmosphere, and Condé's Restaurant for soft-lit, elegant dining. Enjoy tea or cocktails at the Gazebo Lounge beneath the skylit lobby atrium.

A walk down the road to the tiny town of Old Greenwich brings you to a pizza place and Beyond Bread, where you can enjoy fresh muffins and drink coffee while inhaling the heady aroma of baking bread. There is also a small health food restaurant across from the pizzeria.

Staying There

The Hyatt Regency in Greenwich is one of the most luxurious hotels we visited. This striking red brick building was once the headquarters of the Condé Nast publishing company. Take a look at the historic landmark tower. Upon entering the lobby, you come across goldfish-filled streams linked by tiny arched bridges, an outdoor cafe with umbrella-topped tables under a canopy of shade trees, and a country gazebo that provides the setting for evening cocktails. The sun's rays pour through the skylight, gleaming off the crystal glasses. Shiney brass railings circle the terraces of the guest rooms that rise above the "stage set" below.

If you decide to make this an overnight stay and check in at the Hyatt before exploring town, you can unwind by the skylit indoor pool, lie back in the Jacuzzi, work out in the fully equipped health club, or relax in your comfortable room decorated in the English Manor tradition. Later in the evening, enjoy piano music and jazz quartets as you sip a cocktail in the Gazebo Lounge.

This short trip will renew you for many weeks to come.

South Norwalk, Ct

. . . artsy flair; turn-of-the-century charm

DAY TRIP; KID-FRIENDLY

Getting There

Take a Metro-North train (212-532-4900) at Grand Central Station to the recently renovated South Norwalk station. Walk down the hill from the station until you reach South Main Street, then turn left. South Main is the beginning of the refurbished downtown area and runs right into Washington Street.

Being There: Then and Now

South Norwalk, or SoNo as it is now called, is a pretty waterside village with plenty of artistic flair. Washington Street, the village's main street, stretches to the banks of Long Island Sound. It has become an enclave of art galleries, interesting shops, and fine restaurants with turn-of-the-century charm.

The town of Norwalk was established in 1640 when its 16,000 acres were bought from an Indian tribe. In the 1920s, this coastal town on the Long Island Sound became a summer resort for wealthy New Yorkers who traveled to its shores on elegant yachts. The town later fell into a state of neglect and South Norwalk's streets were lined with dilapidated factories. In the 1970s, a group of artists who appreciated the unusual iron-front buildings on South Main and Washington Streets began to restore them. The buildings are now on the National Register of Historic Places.

Seeing and Doing

Meandering through SoNo is a lovely way to spend a day. The best browsing areas in this picture-book town are on South Main and Washington Streets. We chatted with a bartender at The Loft on South Main, who told us he chose to live in South Norwalk because it reminds him of the English village where he spent his childhood.

Children love SoNo's wonderful Maritime Center (203-852-0700), which has an aquarium at the water's edge, around the corner from Washington Street at 10 North Water Street. The aquarium has exceptional exhibits of sea animals, where you can touch living specimens, and features ten-foot-long live sharks (not for touching!) and three daily seal feedings. The Maritime Center holds a winter creature cruise and a holiday hands-on crafts activities celebration dealing with all things related to the sea. The biggest surprise at the center may be the multi-story screen in the IMAX theater, where dramatic documentaries are shown.

SoNo sponsors a number of seasonal celebrations. Every September an Oyster Festival, with tall ships as the backdrop, comes to town. Crafts, food, and, of course, oysters prepared in a number of ways, make this a delicious experience. SoNo also has a river rowing club that offers coached rowing lessons for anyone over 15 years old, on weekends from April through September. For information about schedules, call Yankee Heritage Tourism (203-854-7825).

Eating There

As you turn the corner from South Main Street into Washington Street, you notice the exuberant Southwestern colors of the Rattlesnake Grill, its window filled with cactus plants in the background and a large lizard-like creature that curves along the glass. Featured are such Southwestern specialties as tortillas, quesadillas, burritos, and margaritas.

At the foot of Washington Street, just before you reach the water, is Donovan's, a landmark tavern that's been serving South Norwalkers since 1889. Photos of prizefighters from past decades hang above patrons either seated at round wooden tables or in booths set with blue-and-white gingham tablecloths. This cozy place is great for a juicy burger and a mug of beer. The San Rialto (also on South Main) serves sumptuous vegetarian entrees with an Italian flair. The Brewhouse (on Marshall and North Main) gives you the opportunity to watch the beer-brewing process and then taste a few samples before you dine on wonderful food.

Currently, there is no lodging within walking distance, but since the SoNo area is developing rapidly, call Fairfield County Tourist Information at 800-866-7925 for information about places to stay the night.

Meanwhile, if you want to take advantage of all SoNo has to offer, you can make several day trips; it's only an hour away.

Bloomfield, N.J.

. . . a New England village in New Jersey

DAY TRIP

Getting There

The DeCamp bus (201-783-7500) to Bloomfield leaves from
Port Authority approximately every 20 minutes and takes you
on a nostalgic ride through a *Leave-it-to-Beaver* neighborhood
and on to a Jersey town with a New England village green—
all within 40 minutes of 42nd Street. Ask the driver to let you
off at Belleville and Broad Streets in front of the old Bloomfield High School.

The Ride

As the bus passes the WELCOME TO CLIFTON, NEW JER-
SEY sign, it moves through a neighborhood of homes from
1950s television. Pristine brick colonials with picture windows are interspersed with cottage-style homes with half-
timbered facades and whimsical peaked roofs. The front
lawns contain lovely little flower gardens and the occasional
white picket fence. The bus weaves through the narrow
streets of commercial pockets and then passes a delightful

midtown park with baseball diamond, picnic tables, and a gushing brook.

Being There: Then and Now

Suddenly you're in the heart of Bloomfield and, as you leave the bus, you enter a town whose lush, tree-shaded village green, complete with a white-steepled church, would make a New England village proud. The Bloomfield Village Green, now on the National Register of Historic Places, dates back to the 1700s, when it was used as military parade ground for soldiers of the Revolutionary War and, later, the Civil War. Many New York City brownstones were constructed of sandstone quarried in Bloomfield and brought by boat across the Hudson River.

Seeing and Doing

Although this town could become a tourist mecca, the main shopping area has not for the most part been gentrified with specialty shops, boutiques, or antiques stores (with the exception of Grandma's Antiques at 174 Broad Street). A four-minute walk down Broad Street and a turn to the right takes you to 65 Washington Street, the site of the Taj Mahal, an Indian shop brimming with colorful clothing, jewelry, and exotic scents.

Relax under the huge shade trees on the village green (visualizing Revolutionary War soldiers in full regalia), meander past the handsome homes nearby, and then enjoy a delicious lunch at the Lunchbox Deli at 176 Broad Street—don't miss the luscious desserts.

Step across the street and visit the well-stocked library on Broad Street, where you can purchase good literature—$.25 paperbacks and $1 hardbacks—from A Book Store Under the Stairs.

Founded in 1868, Bloomfield College makes its home here, and many campus buildings are interspersed through the main streets. Two include the Student Organization Headquarters, a red-brick Victorian delight (at 198 Liberty Street), and Webster Hall, a European-style castlelike building with many levels and turrets. Webster Hall houses the college theater and a student art gallery which is open to the public and is located at Franklin and Freemart Street, close to the village green.

Chatham, NJ

. . . a living tribute to Norman Rockwell

DAY TRIP; KID-FRIENDLY

Getting There

New Jersey Transit trains (201-762-5100)—Gladstone Line—depart every hour from Penn Station and arrive in Chatham 30 minutes later. When you leave the train at Chatham Station, walk down Railroad Plaza North Street toward a grassy square, complete with a gazebo. Turn left at Fairmont Avenue onto Main Street. New Jersey Transit buses leave frequently from Port Authority. Call 212-564-8484 for schedules.

Being There: Then and Now

Tree-shaded Main Street looks much like Norman Rockwell's world of the 1940s and 1950s. The street bustles with a variety of shops and restaurants.

Chatham is a perfect place to take children for a day trip. Not only is it a well-preserved, living picture of Americana, but the kids can really enjoy themselves. There is a children's bookstore, an old-time luncheonette with big wooden booths, a homemade ice cream parlor, a sport shop featuring the latest winning team's sweatshirts, and a pet shop with every kind of pet—from dogs and cats to hedgehogs and chinchillas.

Seeing and Doing

Strolling down Chatham's Main Street and Passaic Avenue is a delightful way to spend a sunny afternoon. There are many shops for both children and adults to explore.

SHOPS FOR CHILDREN

Jabberwocky sells games and toys and carries a line of books for teens and young adults. Altered State, "a collector's dream," sells early comic books and specializes in hard-to-find trading cards, action figures, masks, and posters. Pet House sells chinchillas and an assortment of other rare pets. Chatham Sport Shop carries a wide variety of sports paraphernalia, including warm-up suits, sneakers, and headgear. All of these shops are on Main Street.

SHOPS FOR GROWNUPS

The Crafter's Cupboard and Yankee Rooster (next to each other on Main Street) offer a wide array of crafts, antiques, and cozy country collectibles. T. M. Ward Coffee Company, at 7 South Passaic Avenue, boasts fine coffees and teas from all over the world. F. B. Garvelson Company, also on Main Street, is a special shop where fresh coffee is roasted all day long. Filled with a dazzling selection of teapots, salt and pepper shakers, sugar bowls, handpainted dishes, and other treasures, the company was established in 1877. It is now operated by the amiable brother-and-sister team of William Maddox and Constance Towart. Constance is the former proprietor of McNulty's, a well-known coffee shop on Christopher Street in Greenwich Village.

Eating There

Mexico Lindo serves traditional Mexican cuisine in a festive diner with 1930s style and décor. Best Little Luncheonette, which serves homemade soups and breads, sports green-and-white checkered tablecloths and has walls covered with signed photo portraits of baseball greats. Chatham Sandwich Shop, an old-time luncheonette that opens at 6 A.M. and closes at 3 P.M., is well worth a visit for its old-fashioned atmosphere.

*   *   *

It's hard to believe that this tiny hamlet, which epitomizes small-town America, is only a half hour away from the bustle of midtown Manhattan.

Long Branch, N.J.

. . . full service spa; oceanfront boardwalk

WEEKEND TRIP

Getting There

Take the New Jersey Transit train (201-762-5100) from Penn Station to Long Branch. If you're staying at the Hilton, the hotel van picks you up at the station—just let the desk clerk know at what time your train arrives when you make your reservation (908-571-4000).

Being There: Then and Now

The Hilton overlooks the Atlantic and a lovely stretch of beach. A beautifully restored boardwalk is perfect for a brisk walk or jog. The indoor swimming pool and Jacuzzi are spacious and restorative. If you want to relax in your room, you have your choice of videos on demand. The lobby has many sitting areas furnished with wicker chairs and tables. There is the casual ambiance of a summer resort.

If you want pampering, the spa is the place. Choose from several half-day packages that include, among other delightful experiences, full-body massages, deep cleansing facials, seaweed half-body wraps, mud masks, and a spa lunch. The full-day and weekend packages add reflexology, full herbal body wraps, deep scalp treatments, and a relaxing walk along the oceanfront. Individual sessions for a facial or massage are available for an additional charge. For more information and brochures on current spa services, call 908-571-4000, extension 250.

Eating There

In the colder months you are dependent on hotel restaurants, which can be pricey, although a pub lunch in the bar area is fairly reasonable. If you visit in spring or summer, the hotel can recommend several moderately priced eating places within walking distance. On Sundays, enjoy a sumptuous prix fixe brunch. It's a luxurious way to end this special get-away—an excursion that should put an end to your winter doldrums.

* * *

On the van trip back to the station, we met two sisters from New York who have been coming to the Long Branch Hilton for several years for a winter weekend respite. They told us that the van drops them off and picks them up from a nearby shopping mall; so if you're interested, you can also include a shopping trip as part of your agenda.

Madison, N.J.

. . . A New Jersey town with European flair

DAY TRIP

Getting There

The New Jersey Transit Gladstone Line (201-762-5100) runs a direct service train from Penn Station to the Madison train depot. Trains run about once an hour, and the trip takes less than 40 minutes. You arrive in Madison directly across the street from the Madison Cinema House where the town begins.

Being There: Then and Now

Madison has the flavor of a European town, with wide tree-lined boulevards, outdoor cafes on Waverly Place, and gas lamps lining its meandering streets. A three-quarter-mile walk up the hill takes you to the classic college campus of Drew University.

Madison has many shops and restaurants, two live theaters, and a unique museum. Every October, Madison celebrates Battle Hill Day with colorful street festivals from Waverly Place to Main Street.

Seeing and Doing

Turn left from the Madison Street Cinema House, and you come upon Waverly Place, a tree-lined boulevard dotted with old-world gas lamps. Along the boulevard, a cluster of restaurants and cafes offer alfresco dining—large round umbrellas provide shade from the sun.

The Playwrights Theater, at 33 Green Village Road, presents year-round dramatic and musical productions featuring Equity performers. Housed in a campus theater at Drew University is the New Jersey Shakespeare Festival. For information about performances and times for both groups, call 201-595-0189.

The Museum of Early Trade and Crafts, once a beautiful old stone library, can be found at the intersection of Main Street and Green Village Road. Pandora's Book Peddlers, at 9 Waverly Place, a multicultural feminist bookstore, is a cheerful and comfortable spot that stocks books written by and about women.

There are also several craft and gift shops in Madison: Art and Design and Chester Crafts & Collectibles sells lovely handmade items. Seasons carries gifts and home accessories. Time After Time is chock full of vintage clothing and jewelry. All shops are on Main Street. San Francisco Clothing, at 4 Green Village Road, sells frilly romantic dresses and costume jewelry. Next door is the Chatham Bookseller, looking very much like an old-fashioned London bookshop.

Eating There

Amalfi Cafe, at 20 Waverly Place, makes its home in a former bank, a massive stone building dating back to the mid-1800s. The cafe has an old-world charm and outdoor seating. It serves Italian-style pastries, sandwiches, and gelato—that fabulous Italian ice cream that contains 30 percent less fat than the standard American version. Poor Herbie's, a pub-style restaurant with a warm wooden interior, is located at 15 Waverly Place. On A Roll, at 50 Main Street, is a pretty Mediterranean restaurant where you select your food from a glass fronted counter. A large wood-burning fireplace warms the room during chilly winter months. Shanghai Jazz, at 24 Main Street, is a dramatic-looking restaurant with outdoor seating. Large Oriental-style umbrellas shade the round tables. Evenings feature a variety of jazz groups.

*   *   *

The village of Madison exudes an air of sophistication surprising to encounter in a small-town American setting.

Milburn, N.J.

. . . way off Broadway at the Paper Mill Playhouse

DAY TRIP

Getting There

New Jersey Transit provides direct train service to Milburn from Penn Station (201-762-5100). Step off the train at Lackawanna Place and walk until you see a huge diner. Cross the street and turn left to Milburn Avenue. To get to the Paper Mill Playhouse, take a short walk up Main Street from the park to the third street light and turn right onto Brookside Drive. The playhouse is in the middle of the block. Or, the Lakeland bus from the Port Authority (212-564-8484) takes you right to the corner of Brookside Drive in Milburn, where you turn right to get to the playhouse.

Being There: Then and Now

Milburn is a busy little suburban town with upscale shops and eateries of all kinds. Along Main Street is a lovely rose garden that leads to a peaceful park. Amble along its winding footpath past meandering streams, a lake, little bridges, and families of floating ducks. Inviting picnic tables are scattered about. But the real raison d'être for this little trip is Milburn's famous Paper Mill Playhouse.

Seeing and Doing

Housed in a cluster of wooden buildings in a cobbled court-yard, The Paper Mill Playhouse is adjacent to a bubbling brook and a darling restaurant. The Playhouse presents top quality musicals and plays, featuring professional actors; ticket prices are much lower than those on Broadway. Their repertoire during the summer of 1997 included a number of Broadway musical hits. Evita was in performance when we visited, and it was marvelous. Thursday is matinee day. For information on programs and tickets, call 973-376-4343.

Eating There

The Carriage House Restaurant, set in a gleaming white stone building, has received many fine reviews. It serves only those who have tickets to the playhouse, and when you make a reservation for a show, you can get information about dining there.

The train station is well within walking distance of the playhouse, but if you are attending an evening performance, have the theater call a taxi to take you to the station after the show. There are no city lights to brighten your path once darkness descends on Milburn.

Montclair, NJ

... cosmopolitan town, Santa Barbara style

DAY TRIP

Getting There

DeCamp bus #33 (201-783-7500) leaves Port Authority for Montclair every hour. The trip takes only forty minutes.

Being There: Then and Now

A settlement at the foot of New Jersey's Watchung Mountains, Montclair was once called Cranetown and was purchased by the English in 1668. In the late 1700s, Cranetown—a village of farmers and shop owners—received a New Jersey land grant, with its liberal political and religious privileges. The enlightened attitude of the population fostered the development of a town well known today for its cultural and ethnic diversity.

Seeing and Doing

When the bus enters Montclair, it continues up Bloomfield Avenue, a hilly road with a multitude of shops and commercial buildings of various architectural styles. The central business district, historically known as Six Corners, is at the intersection of Church Street, Bloomfield, and North and

South Fullerton Avenue. Here you find tree-lined streets with antique shops, cafes, nostalgia shops, and the wonderful Montclair Book Center, at 219-221 Glenridge Avenue, which sells bestsellers as well as out-of-print books.

You can get off the bus at Church Street, or ask the driver to drop you at the Montclair Museum of American Art, New Jersey's first public museum. In a wooded setting at the corner of Bloomfield and South Mountain Avenue, this neo-classical building houses works by American artists from the eighteenth century to the present, including George Innes (who lived in Montclair in the late 1800s), John Singer Sargent, James McNeill Whistler, Georgia O'Keeffe, Robert Motherwell, and Willem DeKooning. When you leave the museum, cross Bloomfield Avenue and wander by the mansions lining South Mountain Road to your left and North Mountain Road to your right. Among them is Evergreen, a beautiful old home recently bequeathed to the town.

Back on Bloomfield, a leisurely walk downhill takes you past many shops and the Screening Zone, an art movie theater at 544 Bloomfield Avenue (201-509-0273). Continue to the Crescent, a shady enclave off Church Street that resembles a California Village. A wide brick walkway with open-air cafes, Church Street is opposite a Mission-style building with a red tiled roof that houses the community theater. You encounter one specialty shop after another on this winding street, including the Outdoor Shop, for camping and athletic gear; Beans, for fine coffee and teas; Toys in the Attic and Dolls in the Attic (across the street), for a large, tasteful selection of old-and new-fashioned gifts for children. Other points of interest include the Essex Fine Arts Gallery at 13 South Fullerton, and Kindred Spirits at 22 South Fullerton which sells crystals for every purpose, beautiful jewelry, gifts, and cards.

Montclair has a lot to offer, including four live theaters and a rapidly growing number of art galleries—so you may want to visit more than once. There is no overnight lodging in town, but since Montclair is only about forty minutes away from New York City, it makes a perfect day trip. Remember to ask the bus driver where to pick up the bus going back to New York—and keep a schedule handy.

May is an excellent time to visit Montclair. The many gardens for which this town is nationally known are glorious at this time of year, and there's a month-long festival celebrating everything from children's events to dance to special exhibits at the art museum. Call the Chamber of Commerce at 201-744-7660 for specifics.

Eating There

Church Street offers a choice of bistros for lunch or snacks. We enjoy The Stock Pot at 20 Church Street, which has outdoor seating and fabulous sandwiches; Raymond's, for great muffins and coffee; and we love Mexicalli Rose at 10 Park Street. On Bloomfield is the casual and friendly Café Eclectic, where you can relax with a magazine, and Cup and Chaucer, featuring a good selection of multicultural books. There are Indian and Asian restaurants, too, and Blue Sky, at number 398, serves inventive American food.

New Brunswick, NJ

. . . home of Rutgers University; world-famous art museum

DAY OR WEEKEND TRIP

Getting There

Suburban Transit buses (800-262-2497) leave from Port Authority every half-hour and stop at Neilson and Albany Streets in the heart of town, just across the road from the sprawling green lawns of the Hyatt Regency, an ideal spot to spend the night. New Jersey Transit trains (201-762-5100) leave frequently from Penn Station and arrive at the newly renovated Victorian railroad station, also in the town center. The trip from Manhattan, by train or bus, takes about 45 minutes.

Being There: Then and Now

Established in 1680, the town lays claim to the New Brunswick Center, a prominent art district of performers, craftspeople, and fine artists. The Center houses the New Jersey State Theater, the American Repertory Ballet, Crossroads Theater Company, and the George Street Playhouse.

Seeing and Doing

As you leave the bus, or walk down Albany Street from the train station, toward the Hyatt, you pass Kilmer Square, home to an intriguing mix of shops, restaurants, and services. Our favorite is Hollywood and Vine, featuring hand-crafted artifacts, gurgling fountains, and Mexican lanterns and mirrors.

Kilmer Square is named for author, poet, and native son, Joyce Kilmer who was born here in 1886. He attended Rutgers University and was killed in action during World War I at the age of 32. The house in which Kilmer grew up is now a museum—tours are held on weekdays (call 908-745-5117 for more information).

A few blocks away, on the campus of Rutgers University, is the Zimmerli Museum, whose permanent exhibits include the largest collection of nonconformist Soviet art outside the Soviet Republics. To get to the Zimmerli, walk up Albany Street till you reach George Street, then turn right and walk alongside the university until you reach the museum at the corner of George and Hamilton Streets. In addition to its permanent collections, the museum offers an ever-changing series of exhibitions, a small cafe, and a charming gift shop.

The New Brunswick Cultural Center, an enclave of theaters and galleries, is at the intersection of Grove and Hamilton Streets. The State Theater (723-246-7469) offers performances nightly throughout the year. The Manhattan Transfer, Bill Cosby, and the National Russian Orchestra all performed there recently. The theater also features performances of the American Repertory Ballet several times a year. Prices are much lower than in Manhattan. For a brochure, call 732-246-7469. The Crossroads Theatre (732-246-7469), at 7 Livingston Avenue, a continuation of Grove Street, is America's preeminent African-American theater and presented the world premiere of *The Darker Face of the Earth*, by Poet Laureate Rita Dove. The George Street Playhouse (732-246-7717) has featured performances of *The Sunshine Boys*, *To Kill a Mockingbird*, and Tom Ziegler's *Grace and Glorie*.

Directly across from the State Theater is New Jersey Designer Craftsmen, at 10 Livingston Avenue, where handmade New Jersey contemporary, traditional, and folk crafts are sold. Nearby on quaint George Street are several antiques shops and the wonderful Pyramid Bookstore, where current paperbacks sell for half price.

If you are visiting New Brunswick during the week and are interested in biblical history, walk back to Rutgers and over to 17 Seminary Place, where the original library of the New Brunswick Theological Seminary—the oldest seminary in the country—is located. Inside its hallowed halls is a collection of Bibles from all over the world. A Romanesque-styled room with clerestory windows is devoted to books of art. The seminary is open to the public only on weekdays. Call 908-247-5243 for hours.

Eating There

The Old Bay restaurant, (reservations recommended—732-246-3111) just across the street from the Hyatt at 61 Church Street, is an authentic recreation of a nineteenth-century New Orleans bistro. Its specialty is highly spiced French-Creole dishes, but a variety of food is available, including prime steak, fish of the day, and award-winning beers from the South. Listen to live blues and jazz while you feast on oyster stew.

Sapporo, at 375 George Street (732-828-3888), which serves fine Japanese food—including sushi and sashimi—is described in the recent *Zagat Survey* as "still undiscovered with great sushi, good value, and lovely service." For lunch or more casual fare, try Harvest Moon Brewery, 392 George Street, (732-249-MOON), which offers creative American food in a unique setting and beers and ales brewed on the premises (with names like Crazy Girl Golden and Sully Oatmeal Stout).

For a tasty lunch, try Old Man Rafferty's, at 106 Albany Street (732-846-6153) where you're encouraged to "Eat dessert first; life is short." Housed in a turn-of-the-century building with a cozy lamplit interior and decorated with newspaper photos of the early days of New Brunswick, it serves casual cuisine such as hamburgers and deli sandwiches. Its adjoining shop, Rafferty's, carries an elaborate assortment of gourmet cheeses, meats, special pâtés, salads, and pasta dishes for take-out. The wine cellar features a wide range from simple Chianti and Beaujolais to the best vintage champagnes.

Staying There

The Hyatt Hotel Regency (at Albany and Neilson, 800-233-1234) is ideally situated for walking to all of the interesting spots in town. Plump-cushioned sofas and chairs are arranged in small clusters in the hotel lobby. Chandeliers provide soft light and soothing notes of live piano fill the air. A glass elevator, framing four different views of the town skyline, lifts you to clean and comfortable guest rooms. Ask for a room with a view of the white-steepled Reformed Church, which dates back to the early 1800s, complete with its churchyard of timeworn headstones.

Princeton, NJ

...gorgeous university town, lovely Palmer Square

DAY OR WEEKEND TRIP

Getting There

Take the New Jersey Transit train (201-762-5100) from Penn Station to Princeton Junction. There, board the little one-car train known as "the dinky" to Princeton Station at the edge of the Princeton campus. The entire trip takes about an hour. Walk up University Place, passed the campus until you come to Nassau Street on your right. Nassau Street leads you directly to Palmer Square, the center of town. Or take a Suburban Transit bus (800-262-2497) from Port Authority to Palmer Square, right in the center of Princeton. The bus trip takes about 15 or 20 minutes longer than the train, but if the weather is less than perfect, taking the bus saves walking to and from the train station.

Being There: Then and Now

The stately towers of Princeton University form a backdrop to this bustling little town founded by Quakers in 1696. During the Revolutionary War, the Battle of Princeton was the site of George Washington's great victory over the British.

Washington signed the peace treaty with England at Princeton, then delivered his farewell-from-the-army address from the balcony of a building that has since been restored and moved to the Princeton campus.

The university has had many notable students including Presidents James Madison, Woodrow Wilson, John F. Kennedy, F. Scott Fitzgerald, Booth Tarkington, Eugene O'Neill, Jimmy Stewart, and Brooke Shields. Nobel Prize winner Toni Morrison teaches there today.

The Princeton Historical Society (158 Nassau Street) sells maps to guide you through this town filled with historical homes and architectural landmarks. Just off Nassau street is Palmer Square, where a cluster of over 50 charming shops surround the historic and beautiful Nassau Inn. Witherspoon Street is another delightful road for shopping and dining. Look for the cobbled alleyways and tiny side streets that give this town its charming ambiance.

Seeing and Doing

For American history enthusiasts, there are a number of points of interest within walking distance of Palmer Square. Bainbridge House, home of the Princeton Historical Society (609-921-6748), is a 1776 Georgian brick house with changing exhibits, a library, and photo archives of Princeton's fascinating history. Princeton Theological Seminary, on Mercer Street, was established in 1812 and is the largest Presbyterian seminary in the United States. (Albert Einstein lived at 112 Mercer Street from 1935 to 1955.)

Mercer Street leads to Princeton Battlefield State Park—a short hike or taxi ride away. The 85-acre park was the site of Washington's victory over the British army in 1777, considered a critical maneuver for the victorious colonists. Morven, on Stockton Street, is an historic landmark built as a residence in the 1750s by Richard Stockton, a signer of the Declaration of Independence. This brick house served as headquarters for British General Cornwallis in 1777, and from 1953 to 1981 was the official residence of New Jersey's governors. Scheduled tours are available on Wednesday from 11 A.M. to 2 P.M. Otherwise, tours are by appointment (609-683-4495).

And last on our historic tour is the Princeton Cemetery (609-924-1369) at Witherspoon and Wiggins Streets, where you can see the headstones of Aaron Burr, Grover Cleveland, Paul Tulane, and John Witherspoon.

Wander the grounds of Princeton University's magnificent campus or, better yet, take a tour (tours leave from Maclean House to the right of the campus gate). Don't miss the university chapel, the third largest in the world, with exquisite stained-glass windows, each created by a different American artist. There are also two marvelous museums on campus. The University Art Museum (609-258-3788), at McCormack Hall, has a permanent collection of art and artifacts from around the world, including a collection of charming American folk art. This light and airy museum features wonderful traveling exhibits as well, and is open Tuesday through Sunday, but closed Mondays and holidays. The Museum of Natural History (609-258-4102) is in Guyot Hall, at Washington Street and Ivy Lane. It is open only on weekdays from 9 A.M. to 5 P.M., and exhibits dinosaurs, fossils, and minerals.

While wandering around the campus, we were lucky enough to come upon students singing a capella under Blair Arch. We learned that a capella contests had been held since Princeton's earliest days at this very spot because of its perfect acoustics.

There is great shopping in and around Palmer Square, Nassau and Witherspoon Streets. Elegant boutiques, craft shops, and fashionable clothing stores are a few of the fine stores you'll discover.

Eating There

A continental or full breakfast and hearty foods for lunch or dinner are served in the pub atmosphere of the Nassau Inn's Yankee Doodle Tap Room, which features one of Norman Rockwell's largest murals, *The Yankee Doodle*. Palmer's, also at the inn, serves classical American cuisine from 6 to 10 P.M., Tuesdays through Saturdays—jackets are recommended for men. Breakfast and lunch menus are offered at Olives Gourmet Bakery and Deli, at 22 Witherspoon Street. Bountiful platters of Italian-style pastas and salads are served for lunch and dinner at moderate prices at Teresa's, just across the road from the Nassau Inn. Quilty's is a charming French bistro at 18 Witherspoon Street (609-683-4771). The family-run Annex Grill, 128 1/2 Nassau Street, is less than two blocks from Palmer Square, and is an inexpensive student hangout that serves pretty good Italian food.

Staying There

Nestled in the heart of Palmer Square, The Nassau Inn (609-921-7500) is a two-century-old colonial lodging house with weathered shingles and dormer windows that sits atop a gently sloping hill of cobbled paths and green lawns. The Nassau Inn's guest rooms feature period furnishings and comfy country quilts. Each guest receives a "sweet dreams" chocolate mint or cookie in the evening. The stone lobby has an immense hearth, where a fire burns in the winter. Red leather highback chairs and couches and multipaned windows enhance the tranquil setting. Even if you're not a guest, stop by to sit by the fire and sip a glass of sherry or red wine.

We also enjoy staying at the Forrestal in Princeton (800-222-1131 or 609-452-7800), a small Scandinavian-style hotel tucked into a wooded area, with a swimming pool and special weekend rates. The proprietors at the Forrestal are very accommodating. They will pick you up at the railroad station on your arrival (about 15 miles away) and transport you back and forth to town, free of charge. You can order lunch in front of a blazing fireplace in a little nook off the main lobby or in the secluded wicker-furnished sunroom.

Princeton has lots to see and do. In order to take it all in, you may need an extended weekend. And if you decide to stay a night or two, you can enjoy an evening of theater at the McCarter Theater (609-683-8000), 91 University Place—right across the street from the railroad station—where professional drama and musical events (some even before they go to Broadway) have been performed since 1929.

Red Bank, NJ

. . . paradise for antiques lovers

DAY OR WEEKEND TRIP

Getting There

Academy Line buses (212-964-6600) leave Port Authority for Red Bank several times a day. The trip takes about an hour. New Jersey Transit trains (201-762-5100) leave regularly from Penn Station. Buses and trains stop at the Red Bank train depot. Built in 1878, this gingerbread-trimmed pink-and-white Victorian structure is a fine example of stick-style design with Gothic revival elements. It is listed on the State and National Register of Historic Places.

Being There: Then and Now

If you love antiques, you'll be soul satisfied after a weekend, or even a day, in this antiques heaven. The Red Bank Antique Center is one of the oldest antique centers in the country. Just a short walk from the bus and train stops, it fills three enormous buildings that were factories during the World Wars (the big red one was a parachute factory), and some smaller frame buildings. Today they're divided into individual shops, where one room after another is filled with every antique and collectible under the sun. Additional shops have sprung up in every available space nearby.

Seeing and Doing

Brimming over with a multitude of unique and wonderful pieces, the Red Bank Antique Center draws shoppers (including a number of major celebrities) from all over the country and around the world. To get to the Antique Center from the train or bus station, cross the street toward Tavern on the Tracks—this brings you to Bridge Street. Walk two short blocks along Bridge Street (pass the Galleria, a beautifully converted factory of lovely shops and eateries where you might want to browse a while) to the traffic light. Now you're on Front Street and the Antique Center is straight ahead.

Eating There

Restaurants, snack shops, and pizzerias are intermingled with antiques stores. The Galleria's elegant House of Coffee faces onto Bridge Street. Up a few steps in the Galleria, overlooking Front Street, is Charlotte's which serves standard American fare. Across from the Galleria you'll find Danny's Steak House on Bridge Street. Try Pasta Grill, a tiny old-fashioned luncheonette on Front Street, which has been run by one family for 65 years.

Staying There

We recommend the Molly Pitcher Inn (800-221-1372), a lovely place rich in history and within walking distance of the train station. Walk up the block from Front Street and the Antique Center to Merton Avenue. Turn right on Merton and then right again on St. John's Place at the traffic light. Cross over to Riverside Avenue. Turn left and walk half a block to the Molly Pitcher. It's a 10-minute walk, or you can grab a taxi at the train station.

Built on the banks of the Nevasink River in 1928 by a group of Red Bank residents and modeled after Philadelphia's Independence Hall, the inn is a striking red brick colonial-style building with white trim. There are several restaurants as well as a pool, and you're treated to a stunning view of the river and its colorful marinas as you dine or sunbathe on the many verandas that overlook the river. When you register, be sure to ask for a room with a view.

Who, you may ask, is Molly Pitcher—the inn's namesake? During the Revolutionary War's 1778 Battle of Monmouth, the temperature was high and caused men to collapse from heat exhaustion. The women who followed the troops to battle to provide fresh water became so frightened of the cannons that they fled the battlefield. Only one woman remained and continued bringing water to the men from a nearby well. Her name was Mary Hays. The men began to yell "Molly, another pitcher!" or just "Molly Pitcher!" Molly's bravery earned her a military pension, once reserved only for men.

Verona Park, NJ

. . . paddleboats and waterside dining

DAY TRIP; KID-FRIENDLY

Getting There

Verona is only 40 minutes from Port Authority by DeCamp
Bus Lines (201-783-7500). The bus stops directly across the
street from the town park at Lakeland Drive, and the return
stop is right in front of the park. Buses run every hour.

Being There: Then and Now

It's a weekend afternoon in Verona Park, New Jersey. You
step onto a winding path, pass a rushing waterfall and a cluster of kids huddled in the thick branches of the "climbing
tree," walk past a children's playground with brightly painted swings, slides, and monkey bars, and come upon beautiful
Verona Lake. Ducks and geese glide gracefully along the sur-
face. Giggling couples and laughing families pump along in
paddleboats. A rambling restaurant at the water's edge sells
hot dogs, sandwiches, and ice cream from its outdoor deck.

Eating There

The Boathouse on the lake serves casual food by day and has an elegant dinner menu recommended by a *New York Times* food critic. Tables and chairs line the deck, and inside the atmosphere is a bit like a summer camp dining hall, with its stucco walls and beamed ceiling. During the winter, a roaring fire in the huge stone hearth warms folks who come to ice skate when the lake freezes over. Just a few strides up the street, on Bloomfield Avenue, is an IHOP (International House of Pancakes), a great treat for youngsters from Manhattan.

Seeing and Doing

Verona Park is a tiny replica of Central Park and, in fact, was designed by the son of landscape artist, Frederick Law Olmsted, who designed both Central and Prospect Parks. This hilly, peaceful oasis spans 50 acres and has paths for jogging, skating, and just meandering. Behind the Boathouse Restaurant, children can play on a tiny stone castle and imagine being fairy tale princes and princesses. It's also great for tennis players (court time is just $3 a half-hour) and those who wish to fish (the lake is stocked with trout). At the Boathouse Restaurant, paddleboats rent for $6 a half hour and for $10 an hour.

Yaohan Plaza, NJ

EDGEWATER

. . . Tokyo on the Hudson

DAY TRIP

Getting There

Go to Gate 51, in the back of the Port Authority Bus Terminal 40th Street building. Tell the uniformed dispatcher that you want the Community Line Van to Yaohan Plaza. Community Line operates modern, air-conditioned, and comfortable minibuses that go right into the Plaza. The one-way trip costs less than $3.

The minibus passes quickly through the Lincoln Tunnel and wends its way along Boulevard East in Weehawken, New Jersey, where the views of the New York skyline are breathtaking. And 20 minutes later, you find yourself in a different world—where every sign, every book, every clothing tag—almost every item that meets your eye—is labeled and described in Japanese.

Being There: Then and Now

Yaohan Plaza is divided into a food plaza, a huge grocery store with Japanese produce, sushi bars, and food courts, and a specialty plaza that houses a variety of shops under one roof, selling books, greeting cards, housewares, boutique items for men and women, children's clothing and toys, jewelry, and a vast collection of other novelty items—all made in Japan. It's a great place to stock up on Japanese cooking ingredients. Most customers are Japanese, as are all clerks and cashiers, so you really feel as though you are shopping in a faraway land.

Eating There

The food court in the supermarket is a great place to pick up sushi and sashimi. You'll enjoy eating at the tables clustered in a glass-enclosed area overlooking the Hudson River.

For more serene surroundings, dine at the Huo Chan Restaurant, a towering enclosure of foliage-covered stone fountains and goldfish ponds with striking window views of the Hudson and the spires of The Cathedral of St. John the Divine on the Manhattan side.

Should you begin to yearn for a dose of American shopping culture, walk just up the road to the Edgewater Shopping Plaza where you'll find many new chain stores.

Chappaqua, NY

. . . quaint village perfect for strolling and shopping

DAY TRIP

Getting There

The Metro-North train (212-532-4900) to Chappaqua takes less than an hour from Grand Central Station and runs frequently. When you leave the train station, turn left to the end of the road where a half-timbered building marks the corner of King Street, the busiest street in town.

Being There: Then and Now

Chappaqua's history dates back to 1696. It is a lovely town to visit—huge trees and rolling hills surround the hub of the commercial district, which stretches from King Street to North Greeley.

A tiny, pristine town, Chappaqua is ideal for strolling, lunching, and shopping (especially for elegant women's clothing and jewelry). There is one antiques shop in the village and, if you have your walking shoes on and are up to climbing hilly King Street, you'll find several more on the hill.

Seeing and Doing

Looking like the center of a country village, King Street is lined with shops, including an old-fashioned barber shop, replete with a spinning red-and-white striped pole and Penny Aunties, a quaint five-and-dime store with an awning. Quality shops for women include Indigo, a lovely boutique featuring velvet and lace dresses, and Aqua which stocks unique at-home outfits, as well as a wide selection of flannel sleepwear decorated with 1940s designs. We especially enjoyed Crafts Marketplace, a huge space filled with clothes, wall hangings, spreads, and metalwork from all over the world.

Around the corner, at 61 North Greeley Street, find Your Opportunity, a thrift and consignment shop, and further down North Greeley is the cozy, well-stocked Chappaqua Bookstore. Heading back toward King Street and down South Greeley Avenue, is Great Stuff, featuring stylish women's clothing, and further down, Duane and Hudson, a large and popular antiques haven.

Eating There

Susan Lawrence, at 25 North Greeley Street, is a gourmet food and cappuccino cafe that serves homemade soups, sandwiches, and delicious pastries at indoor and outdoor tables. The Chappaqua Restaurant and Coffee Shop, at 105 South Greeley, has the feel of an old-time luncheonette, with turquoise upholstered booths and a soda fountain. Pizza Station, at 88 South Greeley Street, provides outdoor seating on a tree-shaded corner and serves pizza and pasta. This is a good last stop before leaving Chappaqua, since it is right across the road from the train station.

Hudson River Towns Trolley

IRVINGTON, NEW YORK

... historic homes and the Legend of Sleepy Hollow

DAY OR WEEKEND TRIP; KID-FRIENDLY

Getting There

Take the Metro-North train (212-532-4900) from Grand Central to Irvington. At the front of the station, board the red trolley to take you to the historic sights. (Call 914-591-7730 for a current trolley schedule.)

Irvington's Main Street is lovely, and if you get to town with an hour to spare before your trolley is scheduled to arrive, there's time to walk up this hilly road and explore its enticing shops as well as the Irvington Art Gallery, which exhibits and sells paintings featuring local scenes. When the trolley arrives, pay $2 and hop aboard.

Being There: Then and Now

The trolley takes you up the hill, past huge mansions that once belonged to rich merchants who came from Manhattan to vacation and sometimes to stay. You can spend a day here, or you can spend a weekend and visit two towns, three major historic sites, and take a boat ride up the Hudson River.

Seeing and Doing

Swans floating on an old mill pond, delicate bridges with Old World charm, a simple white stone house with a shingled roof and shuttered windows, a weathered wooden barn, rolling meadows, winding paths, and men and women dressed in colonial costumes—this is the view of Phillipsburg Manor, as seen from the veranda of an airy cafe on the grounds of this historic eighteenth-century farm. If you cross the bridge next to the cafe, you come to a huge herb and vegetable kitchen garden, adjacent to the manor house, then a fenced pasture of grazing cows. Welcoming you may be the farm rooster who sits on a fence. Look up at the hayloft in the old barn and down at the beautiful Dutch hens called Penciled Hamburgs. Outside, the shaded meadow is crowded with sheep, goats, and more of those great looking hens. Don't miss the demonstrations of open-hearth cooking, cheese making, spinning, and weaving. A tour of the manor house with its authentic two-century-old furnishings is also worthwhile.

Back on the trolley, you travel through Tarrytown down to the Hudson where, at 1 P.M., you can cruise on a riverboat to Poughkeepsie and back. If you take the boat ride, the trolley will be waiting when you return. If you don't choose to cruise, let the trolley take you along Tarrytown's charming Main Street, lined with shops and restaurants, where you can hop off for lunch. After you reboard, visit the dramatic Lyndhurst Mansion, and then the home of writer Washington Irving at Sleepy Hollow (admission to each is about $8).

Resembling a small castle, Lyndhurst Mansion is set back on verdant rolling meadows surrounded by tall shade trees. Once the home of Jay Gould, the railroad magnate, it's a fine example of Hudson River Gothic architecture from 1880. Left to his daughter, Helen Gould Shepard, the estate was the setting of her elaborate parties on the great lawn. When she died, the family bequeathed Lyndhurst to the National Trust for Historic Preservation.

The last trolley stop is Sunnyside, home of Washington Irving, famous for his stories "Rip Van Winkle" and "The Legend of Sleepy Hollow." Irving loved the Hudson River valley and bought this little farmhouse on the river in the 1830s. Through the years, he expanded and remodeled his house, adding architectural details such as tiny steps that run up and down the gabled roofs, while keeping the interior decor snug and simple. He shared his home with his niece, servants, and many guests. As you tour the grounds you'll discover an icehouse, a woodshed, root cellars, tranquil gardens, and a lovely orchard.

Eating There

The Tarrytown Hilton has three dining places: a pub where you can drink draft lager and eat fresh popcorn while you watch the latest sports events; the Dutch Treat coffee shop, which serves an informal meal; and the elegant Pennybridge restaurant, which offers a menu of Continental specialties for dinner and a champagne brunch every Sunday. Or discover one of a number of good cafes and restaurants in Tarrytown along the trolley route.

Staying There

If you decide to stay for the weekend, we recommend the Tarrytown Hilton (800-HILTONS or 914-631-5700). The trolley stops in front of the hotel, so you can take it from the train station, check in, and, a half hour later, pick up the trolley again for your journey through Sleepy Hollow.

This sprawling red brick hotel complex, surrounded by acres of rolling countryside, has the ambiance of a large country inn—in fact, the guest rooms are decorated in a country motif. A cheery fireplace and baskets of fresh red apples welcome you to the lobby. The more athletic among you will be happy to hear that the hotel has both an outdoor and indoor swimming pool. Every evening after 9 P.M., there is dancing to live music in the Snuggery Lounge.

Long Beach, LI

NEW YORK

. . . easy ocean getaway

DAY TRIP; KID-FRIENDLY

Getting There

Take the Long Island Rail Road (718-217-5477) direct to Long Beach from Penn Station. There is no need to change trains. The train passes many waterways as you get closer to Long Beach, and the pretty ride makes an enjoyable part of a great beach day. When you buy your train ticket, ask to purchase your beach pass along with it.

Being There: Then and Now

Long Beach is the only beach town that you can get to directly by the Long Island Rail Road within an hour's time. Restaurants and shops line the main streets, and the station is only two short blocks from the beach. Walk down Edward Boulevard, or choose one of the less crowded streets parallel to it. The beach entrance from Edward Boulevard has a bathroom (cleaned every day) that opens onto the boardwalk. There are no changing rooms, rental chairs or umbrellas, so bring your own light chairs with umbrellas that hook to the sides. There is no shade.

The boardwalk is wide, the sand is clean and white, and the ocean is beautiful. You may want to bring a sandwich from home as there is only snack food on the boardwalk, or pick up lunch from one of the several delis near the railroad station.

Unique to Long Beach are the wonderful 1940s stucco Hollywood-style homes along its side streets. Wander these streets, if you can stand to leave the beach, and amble by houses with a movieland glamour generally not seen in these parts.

Old Bethpage Village, LI

NEW YORK
... restored colonial village

DAY TRIP; KID-FRIENDLY

A Visit to Old Bethpage Village
A real-life fable by Susan Clemett

Once upon a time there was a little girl named Vanessa who often came to visit her grandmother, who lived in Susan's building. One fine fall day Susan asked Vanessa if she would like to go to the Pumpkin Festival at Old Bethpage Village on Long Island. Vanessa said sure, and off they went to Penn Station to take the Long Island Railroad (718-217-5477). They boarded the train to Port Washington station, where they got off and took a short cab ride to an enchanting reconstructed colonial village.

They entered Old Bethpage through a gift shop filled with reproductions of colonial artifacts. Tin lanterns, silver candlesticks, and homey quilts were among the many treasures for sale. Then, like magic, Susan and Vanessa stepped through a door and out into an eighteenth-century farming hamlet. "Wow," Vanessa said, as they ambled along a wide dirt road past a cornfield and into a tiny one-street village,

"This is like going through a time machine."

"You know," Susan said, "lots of these buildings are really very old and were brought here from other parts of Long Island. People really lived and worked in many of these houses and shops."

"Cool," said Vanessa, and she skipped past the village tavern (they would return later for a cold drink) and popped into the tiny blacksmith shop and then into the general store. Ladies and gents, dressed as they used to in those bygone days, smiled and offered to show them around.

Just then a horse and wagon pulled up. "This will take you to our church and schoolhouse," said a farmer's wife, and Susan and Vanessa climbed aboard. They visited the white clapboard church and the one-room schoolhouse at the top of the hill.

"Life was so different then," sighed Vanessa.

"That's true," said Susan. "But people are still the same and still do the same things—work hard, shop, cook, and take care of their families."

Then they climbed back on the old wagon which rolled down the hill and through the village to a little fenced in farm with horses and cows and lambs.

"I'm having a wonderful time," Vanessa said.

"Glad you are enjoying it," said Susan. "Ready to pick out a pumpkin?"

"Ready," said Vanessa. "Can I get one for Grandma?"

"Of course," said Susan. And they walked toward a patch of bright orange pumpkins.

For information about hours, admission prices, and special events, call 516-572-8400.

Ossining, NY

. . . outstanding architecture and a touch of Portugal

DAY TRIP

Getting There

Take the Metro-North Hudson Line (212-532-4900) from Grand Central Station. The ride along the Hudson is spectacular at any season, but particularly in autumn, when the Palisades on the Jersey side of the river are ablaze with color. When you leave the train station at Ossining, walk down the ramp to Water Street, to the right of the parking lot. This short street takes you to the steep pavement of Main Street, reminiscent of the sidewalk hills of San Francisco. Turn right on Main, keep walking, and after passing a few homes and commercial buildings, you'll come upon a row of architecturally outstanding and beautifully restored structures at the heart of the village. The climb takes about eight minutes, but if you're not in the mood for a short hike, there are always plenty of taxis at the station. Ask the driver to drop you off at the top of the hill.

Being There: Then and Now

For many, Ossining is synonymous with Sing-Sing Prison, but the village of Ossining, across the train tracks and up the hill, certainly bears no resemblance to the infamous slammer. Its main street of handsome, three-story, brightly painted, and extensively refurbished brick buildings date back to the mid-1800s and put Ossining on the Westchester County list of historic landmarks. Ossining also boasts a serene and leafy street of colorful eighteenth-century Victorian homes and a unique gallery of antiques, sculptures, and photographs. But it's also a multiethnic town, reflected in its Portuguese and soul food restaurants and a splendid African boutique.

Seeing and Doing

The restored buildings, some from the mid-nineteenth century, are embellished with ornate cornices, rounded roofs, and scalloped windows. Walkways, shaded by towering elms and maples, weave around the center of the village.

Take a stroll along Ellis Place, a street of lovingly restored Victorian homes. To get there, walk up Main Street toward the white-steepled red brick church towering over the village of Ossining, until you reach a crossroad at the top of the hill. Walk to the left of the church, past the bank on the corner, and cross Highland Avenue. On your right is the street sign for Ellis Place. Most of the houses are adorned with splendid architectural features such as turrets, mansard roofs, garrets, and cupolas. "The Three Sisters' Houses" are identical homes built between 1875 and 1877 in the popular neogothic style. They were designed for Birdie, Margaret, and Edith—daughters of John O'Brien—who owned the store and monument works on Water Street.

Wander back along Main Street, and you'll enjoy Books & Things, a bookstore adjoining a cafe. With wall-to-wall carpeting, it is comfortably furnished with chairs that invite leisurely browsing. Twice Upon a Time, full of delightful surprises, sells gently worn children's clothing, odds and ends, and old-fashioned toys. The Dressing Room, located where Main Street turns toward the left, features West African and Ethiopian ceremonial clothing, masks, jewelry, and unique artifacts. The Hudson River Gallery, housed in a handsome 1870s building, offers beautiful oil paintings, handmade jewelry, and crafts.

Eating There

On Main Street is Lisboa a Nort, a Portuguese restaurant housed in one of the first nineteenth-century buildings you encounter in the town center. Next to Books & Things is Cafe Belem, a simple cafe that sells sandwiches, cappuccino, and delicious homemade desserts. Further up Main Street is Parise's Steak House, where steak is only one of its many specialties. In good weather you can eat outside on the terrace, which looks out on the shady red brick pathway over the Croton Aqueduct.

On Spring Street (which crosses Main), try the E&W Cafe, a simple spot with comfortable wooden booths and benches that serves soul food and Caribbean fare. And stop into Churrasqueira Ribatejo, a cheerfully decorated Portuguese bistro with a white-tiled floor and flower-filled windows.

* * *

The village of Ossining, with its distinctive ethnic flavor, old-fashioned streets, emphasis on the arts, and accessible, lovely strolls along the historic aqueduct, is one of the most interesting small towns we have explored in our travels.

Rye, N.Y.

... old-fashioned amusement park featured

in the movie **Big**

DAY TRIP; KID-FRIENDLY

Getting There

Take the Metro-North train (212-532-4900) from Grand
Central. The trip to Rye takes about 45 minutes. When you
get off the train, you will be facing Purchase Street, the
main street in town.

Being There: Then and Now

If you think Rye looks like a New England village, it's
because it once was a New England village. It belonged to
Connecticut before it was annexed by New York State in the
late seventeenth century as part of the resolution of a bound-
ary dispute between the Dutch and the English.

An authentic colonial tavern, known as the Square
House when it was built in 1760, sits on the edge of the Village Green at the start of Purchase Street. In the late 1700s,
Dr. Ebenezer Haviland took ownership and renamed the tavern the Haviland Inn, attracting customers from George

Washington to John and Samuel Adams. All along Purchase Street are quaint old woodframe houses that have been converted to shops and cafes.

Seeing and Doing

The Square House, on Purchase Street, right near the railroad station, is headquarters for the Rye Historical Society and Museum. Free guided tours are available; call 203-967-7588 for schedules and for the booklet describing Rye's landmark buildings. A beautiful example of colonial architecture, the former tavern is a shingled, gambrel-roofed structure built around a 12-foot-wide chimney. A handsome porch runs the length of the building. You can tour the tavern room, a wonderful colonial kitchen, and the inn's bedrooms—all on one side of the chimney. The other side of the chimney holds meeting rooms, a counsel chamber, and even a grand ballroom.

Check out the shops on Purchase Street, including Chico's—a chain store we always enjoy that sells very stylish, comfortable clothing and beautiful costume jewelry.

Rye is also famous for Rye Playland, an old-fashioned amusement park that was featured in the movie, *Big*. To get there, take the #74 bus from the railroad station. The art deco-style park features an 82-foot Dragon Coaster, one of the few wooden roller coasters left in the country. There are 44 more rides, including a separate area with rides for toddlers and preschoolers called Kiddieland. There is also a pool, a small beach and paddleboats—and you can even play a round of miniature golf and stroll along tree-shaded lanes while munching on candy apples.

Eating There

There are a number of appealing cafes and restaurants to choose from on Purchase Street. Cafe Segale, an Italian bistro, is the first restaurant you come to when you leave the train station. It's open every day but Sunday from 11 A.M. to 11 P.M. Jun & Hoe, at 55 Purchase Street, serves generous meat, cheese, and vegetable sandwiches on oven-baked bread, homemade soups, gourmet salads, and pastas. Farther along, at the corner of Elm Street, is a Starbucks. Turn the corner and you'll discover Mezzaluna, a pizza and pasta restaurant, at 7 Elm Street, with an outdoor cafe to enjoy in warm weather. Across the street at 4 Elm is Longfords, an ice cream parlor where all the ice cream is homemade, using fresh fruits in season. In summer, you can get cantaloupe ice cream and sorbets made with every berry known to humanity. Kids' favorite, as of last summer, was the Oreo bombe; adults love crème caramel.

*   *   *

Summer memories of merry-go-round music, cotton candy, the weathered wooden boardwalk, and the sun sinking down into the waters will keep you warm for many winters to come.

Snug Harbor, NY

... a cultural center on Staten Island

DAY TRIP; KID-FRIENDLY

Getting There

Until Snug Harbor installs its own ferry system, you have to take the Staten Island Ferry and then catch the #72 bus that travels down Richmond Terrace and stops right across the street from Sailor's Snug, at 1000 Richmond Terrace. It's about a 15-minute ride from the ferry.

Being There: Then and Now

Located on Staten Island, just a ferry and short bus ride "across the pond" from Manhattan, the majestic white marble buildings of Snug Harbor are part of a cultural enclave of arts and sciences. Call 718-448-2500 for a brochure detailing the various attractions.

Snug Harbor includes 28 historic buildings on 83 acres of parkland. The restoration and preservation of this nineteenth-century Greek Revival, Beaux Arts, Second Empire, and Italianate architecture is the largest project of its kind in the country today. In the process of opening a restored 1892

Music Hall, Snug Harbor is constructing its own ferry landing that will provide direct service to and from Manhattan.

Seeing and Doing

Currently you can enjoy the Newhouse Center for Contemporary Arts, featuring abstract paintings and sculpture; The Staten Island Children's Museum; The Staten Island Botanical Gardens Art Lab—which offers both courses and exhibitions; a charming duck pond; and a gift shop. Just a few of the events listed in the catalog include evening and afternoon jazz performances, classical music concerts, art discussions, bluegrass and banjo contests, children's theater, and book fairs.

Eating There

You can get a bite at the Manhattan or Staten Island Ferry terminal (pizza, franks, knishes), or you can eat at Melville's Cafe, on the grounds of the Cultural Center. You may also bring along a picnic to enjoy on the grounds—just don't be surprised if the ducks join you.

Van Cortlandt Manor, NY

... the legacy of the Dutch

DAY TRIP; KID-FRIENDLY

Getting There

Take the Metro-North train (212-532-4900) from Grand Central Station to Croton-Harmon. Walk through the station parking lot, where you can get a taxi or go up the stairs to start your 15-minute walk east along Croton Point Avenue. Walk under the overpass (Route 9) until you reach Riverside Avenue. Turn right at the shopping center and follow the road, which brings you directly to the Manor. The visitors' lounge, where you pay for admission, is just past the Manor House.

Being There: Then and Now

Van Cortlandt Manor (914-631-3992) was purchased in 1680 by Stephanus Van Cortlandt, a Dutchman who arrived in New Amsterdam in 1638. Only a one-story hunting lodge when Van Cortlandt acquired it, the manor evolved over the years into a three-story home of brick and clapboard with a generous wood-planked front porch. A cobbled walkway, called "the long path," stretches past orchards and gardens. This path takes you to the Ferry House, formerly a colonial tavern that provided food and shelter for travelers who came by ferry across the Croton River or via the Old Albany Post Road. George Washington used the Ferry House as an outpost during the Revolutionary War.

Seeing and Doing

As you walk through the Ferry House, you can imagine colonial folks catching up on local gossip, eating, drinking, and resting in the front parlor, taproom, and sleeping rooms.

Stroll back to the main house during spring or summer, and costumed guides will escort you to demonstrations of blacksmithing, cooking, weaving, and sheep shearing. You can tour the eighteenth-century rooms of the manor house, where the kitchen bustles with demonstrations of baking bread in beehive ovens and cooking food with colonial utensils. It's a world away, but only an hour from Grand Central Station.

Eating There

A cafe on the manor grounds serves buffet-style. You can also purchase sandwiches and bring them out to the picnic area on the meadow.

Travel Notes

One

and a

Half

to

Two

Hours

Cannondale Village, Wilton

CONNECTICUT

. . . home on the grange

DAY TRIP

Getting There

Take Metro-North (212-532-4900) to South Norwalk, and then switch trains to the Danbury line (on the same track) for the ten-minute ride to the Wilton Station.

Being There: Then and Now

In the 1850s, at the behest of Mr. Cannon, owner of the local general store, the Danbury rail tracks were built to bring trains directly into Cannondale. As farmlands vanished, the townsfolk left the area, leaving behind the sturdy old buildings in which they had lived and worked. Decades later, these were refurbished to become Cannondale Village.

Once a farming village with a post office and general store, Cannondale also had a grange, a wooden structure where farmers and their families came together to trade secrets and learn sewing, baking, and crafts. The grange in Cannondale Village exists today as a showcase for the tradition. There is a grange fair every August, and the Blessing of the Animals is held at the grange every Christmas.

The town held title to Wilton's one-room schoolhouse until the building was sold for $1 to actress June Havoc, sister of Gypsy Rose Lee. Ms. Havoc, who already owned the charming retail complex called Cannondale Village, moved the schoolhouse there and turned it into a tea room. In 1991, Tom King and his daughter, Marcia, bought it and converted it into a restaurant—the Old Schoolhouse Grill.

Seeing and Doing

Built as a rail depot in 1892, Wilton's train station is now called St. Benedict Guild and offers books and unique gifts from around the world. There is an ever-changing art exhibit in an upstairs loft, and the shop downstairs sells coffee and newspapers in the mornings (all profits go to the St. Benedict Monastery). Nearby, are more shops in a bright pumpkin-colored barn. Annabel Green sells exquisite flower arrangements, boutique clothing, and jewelry; Penny Alta features food and crafts from the British Isles; Green Willow Antiques sells a variety of collectibles, from folk art objects to more formal furniture; the Cannondale Art Gallery showcases local and regional artists; and the Well-Dressed Basket is the tiniest gift shop imaginable—it opens onto a shady lawn with a wooden picnic table out front.

Cannondale Village is a great place to treat a friend (say, on a birthday) to a Sunday brunch in warm weather, and maybe a gift certificate for one of the shops. Shop hours are from 11 A.M. to 5 P.M., Tuesday through Sunday. For more information call 203-762-8617.

Silvermine Tavern, New Canaan

CONNECTICUT

... sixteenth-century inn in the lush
Connecticut countryside

WEEKEND TRIP

Getting There

Metro-North takes you to New Canaan. (You have to change trains at Stamford—the train to New Canaan will be waiting at the station.) If you travel light, you may want to explore New Canaan for an hour or two before you catch a taxi from the station (Canaan Parish Taxi, 203-966-6866) for the four-mile, $8 trip to the Silvermine Tavern.

Being There: Then and Now

If you do decide to wander around New Canaan, a tree-lined town of elegant shops, art galleries, beautiful antiques shops, and two exquisite churches, turn right as you leave the station, which brings you to Elm Street, where the town center begins. Walk up Park Street (which cuts right into Elm Street near the station) and climb the hill to "God's Acre," for a closer look at the town's two perfectly classic New England churches.

Once you get to Silvermine, you find yourself in a small pre-Revolutionary War town dating back to 1642. Silvermine no longer has a town center, but its mainstay is the Silvermine Tavern and the Silvermine Guild of Artists, a group of wooden buildings that house a renowned art school and several galleries. The area is famous for its gorgeous scenery, where old stone walls line country roads that wind past ponds, woods, and beautifully preserved old New England homes.

The Silvermine Tavern (203-847-4558), which looks out on the Silvermine River, is made up of a group of five clapboard and shingled buildings. The main one was once the tap room for men working the mills along the river in the mid-1800s. The old mill, located down by the waterfall, was a wood-turning and peg-making factory. The coach house is said to have been used as a still during Prohibition. The former gatehouse now serves as the main dining room. A nineteenth-century country store has been moved onto the site from where it was first built across the road. During its heyday, the country store played many roles. Originally a general store with supplies for the townspeople, it later became a church hall, then a blacksmith shop, and finally a dance hall.

In the early 1900s, the hamlet of Silvermine was home to a community of writers and artists who started the Knockers Club, which later developed into the Silvermine Guild—one of the oldest art centers in New England. When Otto Goldstein bought the tavern for his home in 1906, it became a gathering place for local artists. J. Kenneth Byard bought the complex after the repeal of Prohibition and renamed it the Silvermine Tavern. Byard's collection of antique furnishings, primitive paintings, and farm implements are on display today throughout the inn.

Seeing and Doing

The inn has a delightful gift shop, set back on a wide lawn with a table and lounge chairs. You can walk up the road to view exhibitions at the Silvermine Art Guild, open daily. At the front desk, pick up a copy of the brochure "A Short Walking Tour of Silvermine." The walk, which is about two miles, takes you down to the river, past farmhouses and along winding lanes.

Eating There

The Tavern is famous for its award-winning New England cuisine—especially its honey buns (continental breakfast featuring these honey buns is included in the room rate), and the Sunday champagne brunch buffet is outstanding. Lunch and dinner are served in a charming dining room. In winter, a fire crackles in a hearth hung with antique pots. In spring and summer, you can also dine on a tree-shaded deck overlooking the mill pond and Silvermine River, where swans and ducks swim nearby.

If you just want a sandwich for lunch, you can walk up Silvermine Road to the Silvermine Deli, which sells fresh muffins and sandwiches as well as daily newspapers. Sit at one of the small tables by the windows that look out on the Silvermine Art School just across the road.

Staying There

In the Tavern's guest rooms, country quilts cover four-poster beds and rag rugs cover the wide-plank floors. You can relax with a book in one of the wingback chairs flanking the colonial fireplace in the wood-beamed parlor. The walls are hung with primitive landscapes and portraits from the original Byard collection.

Room rates are moderate: One person can stay for $65; two for $90–110. A third person in the same room is $18 additional. When you call to reserve your room, ask about menu prices, also reasonable.

Flemington, NJ

. . . famous factory outlets; Americana main street

DAY OR WEEKEND TRIP

Getting There

Take the Transbridge bus (800-962-9135) from Port Authority and ask the driver to let you off at the courthouse so you'll have a chance to wander through the town before your shopping begins. To reach Liberty Village, the sprawling cluster of discount shopping outlets for which Flemington is known, turn left at the courthouse on Main Street, then turn right onto Church Street, and walk a block or two until you spot the colonial-style shops. The bus for New York picks up passengers at a little gray building at the edge of Liberty Village off Church Street, just behind the shops Shady Lamps and Bagmakers. For more information, call Hunterdom County Travel at 908-735-5955.

Being There: Then and Now

If you're in the mood to do some exploring and shopping, Flemington can satisfy both desires. The village of Flemington is a perfect example of an American small town. Its streets are dappled with sunshine, which is filtered through the oaks and maple trees that canopy the sidewalks. The Hunterdon County Courthouse, a Greek Revival building dating back to 1828, was the scene of the notorious trial in 1935 in which Bruno Hauptmann was sentenced to death for the kidnapping and murder of aviator Charles Lindbergh's son.

Seeing and Doing

Flemington is a good place to soak up the pretty town atmosphere, lunch in a cafe along Main Street, and move on to shop. There are at least 80 shops in Liberty Village, many of which are outlets for famous manufacturers, and you can busily browse or shop there for hours. The town itself is home to great antiques marts and individual shops and is a wonderful place to find vintage and collectible pottery. Two annual shows are a must—the All-American Pottery and Dinnerware Show and Sale and, in October, the All American Antique Collectible and Pottery Show. For dates and exact details, call Bob Penzel, the owner of Popkorn Antiques, at 908-782-9631, located at 4 Mine Street at the corner of Main.

Eating There

The Union Hotel, directly across from the courthouse on Main Street, is a lovely place to lunch. Built in 1877, this four-story brick building with its mansard roof and gingerbread porches was a popular gathering place during the Lindbergh trial. At that time, it provided lodging as well as food, but today it only serves as a restaurant.

Staying There

Cabbage Rose (908-788-0247), on Main Street, is a Victorian-style bed and breakfast decorated with floral wallpaper and rich furnishings. It has a guest parlor that serves complimentary refreshments which include sodas, ciders, and fruit juices; an oversized cookie jar filled daily with a variety of home-baked cookies; handmade chocolates; and sips of sherry every evening.

Frenchtown, NJ

... enchanting B&B in a village on the Delaware

DAY OR WEEKEND TRIP

Getting There

Transbridge buses (800-962-9135) from Port Authority go directly into Frenchtown and stop at the corner of Bridge Street. Turn right on Bridge Street and you come to the Hunterdon House, which marks the center of town. The ride takes approximately two hours.

Being There: Then and Now

Surrounded by rolling farmland and wooded hills, this small river village on the banks of the Delaware was once a busy mill and farming center. The presence of interesting antiques shops and gourmet eateries give Frenchtown an air of sophistication. If you want a weekend away in a spectacular bed and breakfast with few distractions, then Frenchtown is the perfect place to visit.

Seeing and Doing

After ambling along Bridge Street, it's fun to walk across the bridge that leads to Pennsylvania, where a roadside stand sells fresh produce, flowers, and pumpkins in season. You can sit on a stone wall at the edge of the river and watch the water. There's also a path that runs along the canal on the Frenchtown side that makes for a lovely morning walk. Some evenings there are jazz performances at the hotel across the street from Hunterdon House.

Eating There

The proprietor at Hunterdon House recommends Loafers American Restaurant for lunch, and for fine dining suggests the Frenchtown Inn and the Race Street Cafe—both are on Bridge Street.

Staying There

Built in 1864, Hunterdon House (12 Bridge Street, 800-382-0375 or 908-996-3632) is a Victorian mansion set back on the main street of this country village. Each guest room is furnished differently, and visitors may choose from seven large double rooms, each with private bath. The William Apgar Room has a working fireplace and a hand-carved cathedral-style queen bed, and the Lillian Apgar Room features a carved Italian four-poster canopy bed and a sitting area overlooking Bridge Street. Every evening in the downstairs parlor, guests are invited to sip a glass of sherry, and every morning a complimentary traditional breakfast is served in the gracious dining room.

Lambertville, NJ

... views of riverbanks; birthplace of bobby pins

DAY OR WEEKEND TRIP

Getting There

Take the Transbridge bus (800-962-9135) from Port Authority. The bus ride, which takes about two hours, carries you past rolling acres of farmland, red barns, and grazing cows. Lambertville is situated just a bridge away from the heart of lovely Bucks County, Pennsylvania.

Being There: Then and Now

A bustling industrial center in the 1800s, Lambertville once employed 3,000 factory workers in the production of wooden wagon wheels, railway cars, and boats. The first bobby pins were manufactured in a Lambertville factory. When the railroads and industry left, Lambertville remained a sleepy but charming hamlet of homes and handsome commercial buildings that now house restaurants, arts and crafts galleries, and antiques shops.

Seeing and Doing

Lambertville can be the first stop on a weekend excursion to

New Hope, Pennsylvania. While New Hope has an extraordinary variety of shops and galleries, it is often crowded with tourists. Lambertville, quieter than its Pennsylvania neighbor, is truly a place to savor as you amble its classic American small-town streets. There is a growing number of antiques and collectibles shops. Pick up a self-guided walking tour of Lambertville at one of the village shops and locate Union Street, where you'll find an old-fashioned five-and-dime store that specializes in antique toys.

If you visit on the last weekend in April, you can take part in the Shad Fest—a celebration of the shads' annual return to the upper Delaware River. This event features shad-hauling and fish-tagging demonstrations, food stands, arts and crafts booths, and more.

Lambertville is famous for its antiques and collectibles flea markets on the edge of town. It's worth the mile and a half walk or finding a ride.

Eating There

Manon (19 North Union Street, 988-397-2596) is a bistro that serves Continental menu lunches and dinners, while Anton's at the Swan Hotel (43 Main Street, 988-397-1960) serves French cuisine. For more casual menus, try Hamilton's Grill, 8 Coryell Lane, and the down-home American food at the American Grill Room on Church Street. There is also a restaurant and bar with etched-glass mirrors and oak Victorian tables at the Inn at Lambertville Station (see below).

Staying There

There are several charming places to spend the night in Lambertville: Bridgestreet House (75 Bridge Street, 609-397-2503), at the foot of the bridge leading to New Hope, is a Victorian inn with cozy guest rooms, pretty gardens, and an outdoor Jacuzzi. The recently restored Lambertville House (32 Bridge Street, 609-397-0200) dates back to 1810 and has 25 guest rooms. Adjacent to the old town train station is the Inn at Lambertville Station (11 Bridge Street, 800-524-1091), a restored building dating back to 1867, when it served as the town's post office and train station. Its 45 rooms are furnished with Victorian antiques and the suites have gas fireplaces.

Ocean Grove, NJ

... the jewel of the North Jersey coast

DAY OR WEEKEND TRIP

Getting There

Academy Line buses (212-964-6600) leave from Port Authority (212-564-8484) several times a day. The 1 3/4-hour ride takes you right to the center of Ocean Grove on Main Avenue.

Being There: Then and Now

Listed on the New Jersey Register of Historic Places, Ocean Grove was founded as a camp meeting ground and seaside resort in the summer of 1869 by the Methodist Church. This particular square-mile section of oceanfront property was selected because it was the one area of the Jersey shore where there were no mosquitoes! Once described as "God's Square Mile of Happiness," Ocean Grove is now often called "the jewel of the North Jersey coast," abounding in flower gardens and tranquil, tree-lined streets.

The houses are of many architectural styles, and those along the ocean are set back at varying angles, allowing unbroken ocean vistas and breezes to reach the town.

Entering the town gates on a summer day, you'll be

transported to another time. Ocean Grove has more Victorian homes than any other town in the United States, from pastel cottages to sprawling turreted mansions. As the bus pulls to a stop on Main Avenue, take notice of the many colorful shops and outdoor cafes ringed with festive umbrellas.

Seeing and Doing

Tent City is still summer housing for more than 100 families. The tents—half canvas, half wooden bungalows with open porches and flower gardens spilling out to a communal back-yard—are set around the Great Auditorium, originally built as the Methodist Church House in 1894. Recently restored, the auditorium stands at the beginning of Ocean Pathway, a broad, grassy "boulevard" that leads to the ocean.

Still the heart of the community's religious programs, the auditorium pulpit has hosted many famous preachers, among them Billy Sunday, Billy Graham, and Norman Vincent Peale. Seven U.S. presidents have spoken there. This acoustically perfect amphitheater, where Woody Allen filmed Stardust Memories, is also the setting for a repertoire of entertainment: Enrico Caruso once performed here, and more recently, Pearl Bailey, Duke Ellington, and Victor Borge brought their talents to the village of Ocean Grove.

It's fun just to walk along the seaside streets, admiring Victorian cottages one after the other. Strolling along Main Avenue, you'll pass clusters of shops and eating establishments, including an old-fashioned hardware store and a bakery, famous for its fresh baked breads and delicious coffee. The Shell Shop offers lamps and frames, jewelry, and mobiles made of seashells. Vintage Ocean Grove memorabilia can be found at Gingerbreads Teas & Treasures. Favorite Things specializes in vintage jewelry, lace accessories, clothing, and penny candy.

Eating There

At the Sampler Inn (28 Main Avenue), the walls are covered with cross-stitch samplers, and hearty meals are served cafeteria-style for under $8. Daily specials, along with the serving times for breakfast, lunch, and dinner, are posted outside on the front porch. Get there early. The lines may be long. The Raspberry Cafe, a block up Main Avenue, serves fabulous fresh fruit smoothies, warm pita sandwiches, homemade soups, muffins, and desserts of the day. Just across Main Avenue is the Moonstruck Cafe, offering elegant dining at candlelit tables indoors and outdoors during both spring and summer.

Staying There

Ocean Grove is a seaside resort. Among the town's many Victorian inns and bed and breakfasts, we recommend the rambling, white-shingled Quaker Inn at 39 Main Avenue (908-775-7525), located right across from the bus stop. It has clean, simple rooms at very moderate prices. Its wide terraces, furnished with wicker rocking chairs and gliders, are perfect for watching the ocean and town activities at the same time.

The lavender Carol Inn (11 Pitman Avenue, 732-502-0303) is set back from a yard resplendent with bright flowers planted by innkeeper Caroline McNeil. Rooms are charmingly decorated.

One of the town's newest Victorian-style hotels, the Ocean Plaza (732-774-6552) sprawls along Ocean Pathway. Painted bright pink with wraparound porches and spectacular ocean views, it has spacious air-conditioned rooms with telephone and TV in each. Breakfast is served each morning at 10 A.M. on the second-floor terrace. It is completely relaxing to lay back on a white wicker lounge and watch the town come alive against the backdrop of the sparkling ocean waves.

Cold Spring, NY

... charming Hudson River village with breathtaking views

DAY OR WEEKEND TRIP

Getting There

From Grand Central Station, the Hudson-line Metro-North trains (212-532-4900) leave for Cold Spring about once every hour. The trip takes about an hour and 20 minutes. The train station is right at the end of Cold Spring's Main Street.

Being There: Then and Now

Cold Spring is right next to the Hudson River. Beginning at a glorious little waterside park, picturesque Main Street is crowded with Victorian homes that clamber up the hill away from the river. Swans glide on the river against the backdrop of striking Storm King Mountain—a sight to lift the heart.

Some say that George Washington named the town after the cooling waters of a local stream. The land of which Cold Spring is a part was given to Adolph Philipse, a Dutchman, in the early 1700s, through a land grant from King William III. It was originally settled by the Wappingers, an Algonquin tribe. A hundred years later, the West Point

Foundry was constructed nearby to assemble parts for New York State's first steam engine. This set the stage for the arrival of the New York Central Railroad and began the steady influx of New York City dwellers, inventors, and entrepreneurs who came to the area to vacation and to start businesses. At the turn of the nineteenth century, immigrants poured into the area to work at the granite quarry at Breakneck Mountain, which supplied the stone for the bases of the Brooklyn Bridge and the Statue of Liberty.

Seeing and Doing

Stroll along Main Street to explore one interesting shop after another. Cobbled courtyards ringed by clapboard houses have become shops with wide front porches displaying elegant collectibles and period furniture. You can rest at the waterfront in an old-fashioned gazebo and watch the river roll by.

If you want to know more about Cold Spring history, visit the Foundry Museum at 63 Chestnut Street, once a schoolhouse for the children of the West Point Foundry workers. It features a restoration of the original schoolroom, a nineteenth-century country kitchen, and the famous painting *The Gun Foundry*, by John Ferguson Weir.

The beautifully restored nineteenth-century mansion Boscobel (914-265-3638) is about three miles away and can be reached by walking. If you're in a hiking mood, walk up Main Street to Peekskill Road and turn right. Walk past the cemetery (on the left) to route 9D until you reach the Plumbush Restaurant; walk along the dirt track (parallel to 9D) to the end; then cross 9D, and you'll see the entrance to Boscobel on the right. Or take a taxi, as we did (Cold Spring

Taxi, 265-4440). Boscobel's furnishings are fine examples of the decorative arts of the Federal period. The mansion is surrounded by gorgeous gardens, an apple orchard, and a lovely picnic area.

Eating There

We heartily recommend North Gate Restaurant, at Dockside Harbor, 1 North Street (914–265-5555). To get there, walk past the park gazebo along a stretch of waterfront lawn, turn a corner to the right, and come upon a plush lawn (we love to walk barefoot here) that reaches to the riverbank and a restaurant with huge windows and a patio for outdoor dining. Here the Hudson flows proudly past majestic cliffs and low mountains; massive freighters and small canoes glide on the sparkline water—it's a perfect spot from which to view the sunset. Below, under a broad white tent, there is a bar offering beer and burgers.

Festive umbrellas surround the old Cold Spring Train Station, which has been converted into a charming cafe for casual indoor and outdoor dining. It's a convenient stop for dinner before catching the train back to New York. Sometimes it's very crowded, so you may want to make reservations when you first arrive in town. You can also find several restaurants and delis (for a picnic lunch in the park) along Main Street.

Staying There

We enjoyed our stay at the landmark Hudson House, a country inn at 2 Main Street (914-265-9355), built in 1832 right on the banks of the river. Open year round, it features two tiers of terraces with views of the water and the Palisades on the opposite shore. The price for each quaint room includes a continental breakfast on weekends and a full breakfast on weekdays. Other bed-and-breakfasts to which we gave a look-see and found appealing were the Pig Hill Inn, 73 Main Street (914-265-9247), and One Market Street, on the corner of Main and Market Streets (914-265-3912).

Kingston, NY

... Holland meets the Wild West

WEEKEND TRIP; KID-FRIENDLY

Getting There

Trailways buses (800-343-9999) go directly into Kingston from Port Authority. The ride is about two hours. To begin exploring Kingston, walk toward Friendly's across the street from the bus station and then cross North Front Street and walk past the Hoffman House Tavern (you can return later for lunch or dinner). Continue along North Front until you come to the historic district. During spring and summer, Kingston has a hop-on-hop-off trolley that carts you to all of the city's highlights.

Being There: Then and Now

Originally settled soon after Henry Hudson sailed upriver to explore, Kingston was the first capital of New York State. Its long history is reflected in many of its lovely homes and commercial buildings that date back to the 1700s. In 1653, when the city was destroyed by the Esopus Indians, Peter Stuyvesant ordered a stockade to be built to contain the prisoners and help ward off future attacks.

If you love American architecture, walk through the Stockade District, where architectural styles from the Dutch stone houses of the 1700s to Colonial, Federal, Italianate Romanesque, and Victorian right up to art deco are all represented.

The trolley will take you to the Round Out, a reconstruction of a lively part of town along the Hudson River, where the once-thriving commercial port of Kingston shipped ice cream, coal, and a host of other supplies downriver to New York City.

Seeing and Doing

When you encounter the historic district, you may experience a sudden feeling of déjà vu that takes you back to the famous shootout in *High Noon*. Restored eighteenth-century wooden and stucco buildings feature overhangs that shelter pedestrians during inclement weather. The style of architecture here is rarely (if ever) found in this part of the country.

Moseying along these colorful streets, poking in delightful galleries and shops is a great way to begin your adventure. Make your next stop the Senate House, at 312 Fair Street. Guided tours of the Stockade District begin here, and this is a good place to pick up maps and brochures. Built in 1676, The Senate House was already a century old when the first court was opened. Only the roof of this rock-solid building was damaged when the British set fire to Kingston during the Revolution. A museum adjacent to the Senate House displays many historical objects from this time.

The three-hundred-year-old Dutch Church, near the Senate House on Fair Street, is open Saturdays from 2 to 4

P.M. and displays, among other documents, a letter George Washington wrote after a visit there. The blurred and mossy headstones in the tiny church cemetery reflect how long ago this town was established.

The Stockade District is your next stop. A network of tunnels that was discovered underneath many of these homes has been identified as part of the Underground Railroad. In fact, Kingston is the birthplace of Sojourner Truth. For a guided tour, call Friends of Kingston at 914-338-5100.

The Roundout Landing and the Hudson River Maritime Center are on the other side of town, but it's easy to get there via the touring trolley. The Roundout has been recreated with great charm. Lacy iron grillwork balconies grace the brick buildings that house antiques shops, boutiques, and restaurants.

There is a lovely small park along the edge of the Hudson. Cruises sail on weekend afternoons and at sunset. For more information call 914-255-6515 or 914-473-3860.

Eating There

We love the Hoffman House Tavern, (914-338-2626) a restoration of an original tavern dating back to the 1600s. This colonial-style stone pub has several cozy small rooms with wide wood plank floors and roaring fireplaces in each setting. Schnellers, at 61 John Street (914-331-9800) is a landmark restaurant, known for its German sausages and schnitzel. In warm weather, you can lunch in its shady garden. The Holiday Inn has several eateries, and of course, there is Friendly's on the corner, a treat for kids who live in Manhattan, where restaurants like this are in short supply.

Staying There

We stayed at the family-friendly Holiday Inn (800-HOLI-DAY or 914-338-0400), just two blocks from the Trailways bus stop and about three blocks from the historic district. Cross the street from the Trailways station toward Friendly's restaurant, turn right, and walk up the block toward the large sign that marks the inn. The large indoor swimming pool (open until 10 P.M.) features comfortable lounge chairs and nearby (but out of hearing range), a kiddy pool, pinball machines, and Ping-Pong tables to keep the kids busy while parents swim or relax. The rooms are simple and clean, and the weekend packages are very affordable.

Nyack, NY

... lively old-fashioned waterfront village

DAY TRIP

Getting There

Take the Red and Tan bus (800-772-3689), which leaves from the George Washington Bridge Port Authority Station at 175th Street. (The A subway will take you directly to the bridge station.) When the bus reaches Nyack, it turns a corner onto North Broadway, Nyack's main thoroughfare. Ask the driver to drop you off at Main Street, in the center of the commercial district.

Being There: Then and Now

The bus ride to the turn-of-the-century village of Nyack is glorious, with stunning homes poised high on hills along the road and steep cliffs that slope down to the Hudson River. Hundreds of boats with bright white sails glide and bob beneath the graceful Tappan Zee bridge, which connects Rockland and Westchester counties.

In Nyack, you step into a charming town chock full of

antiques stores, art galleries, and eighteenth-century buildings with cafes and shops featuring avant-garde clothing, crafts, jewelry, and collectibles.

Nyack takes great pride in its abundance of showpiece Victorian homes—brightly painted, ringed with balconies, topped with turrets, and embellished with gingerbread trim. The ground floors of a number of these homes have been turned into shops. It's delightful to wander among them.

Actress Helen Hayes made Nyack her home, and native-born Edward Hopper lived and painted in this charming town.

Seeing and Doing

Nyack is a town for strolling on leafy streets and venturing into interesting shops. Pick up *The Village Guide and Walking Tour*, available in most shops, which leads you down hilly paths to a beautiful stretch of the Hudson River.

If you're in the mood for a bit of a hike, walk along North Broadway toward Hook Mountain State Park, where mansions overlook the sweeping Hudson and sheep graze in a meadow. On North Broadway is an old-fashioned deli—a good stopping point if you plan to picnic in the park. Your hike along North Broadway may also include a visit to Edward Hopper's childhood home, which has been converted into an impressive art gallery.

Nyack has several annual fairs. Call the Chamber of Commerce (914-353-2221) for dates. Note that during these special events, bus schedules and pick up spots may vary (call Red and Tan at 800-772-3689 for more information).

Eating There

Broadway and Main Street offer a variety of restaurants, pubs, ice-cream parlors, coffee shops, cafes, and health-food restaurants. We particularly like the delicious Mexican food at Cafe Sol, on Main Street, with its tiled floors, fanciful iron grillwork, and splashing fountains, reminiscent of charming courtyards in Mexico and Spain.

Staying There

Although there are no accommodations for tourists in town, a day trip to Nyack is still a delightful adventure.

Piermont, NY

. . . gussied-up 1930s town where Woody Allen

filmed the **Purple Rose of Cairo**

DAY TRIP

Getting There

Take the Red and Tan bus line (800-772-3689) that leaves from the Port Authority station at the George Washington Bridge at 175th Street. The A subway line will take you to 175th Street and the GWB building. The bus leaves about once every hour.

You can take the bus directly to Piermont, or if you're in the mood for a walk (about one mile), ask the driver to let you off at Sparkhill, the town before Piermont, so that you can stroll alongside the enchanting Sparkhill Canal. When you reach the end of the canal, you pass Tallman State Park, a hilly woodland of nature trails with picnic tables, and a swimming pool, about a quarter mile from the main road. To keep walking to Piermont, cross the tiny wooden bridge that overlooks a reedy Hudson River inlet where small rowboats are docked. Once you pass the adjoining children's playground you find yourself in the village of Piermont, with its network of narrow roads meandering up the hillside.

Being There: Then and Now

Nearly unchanged since the 1930s, Piermont is the tiny town on the Hudson River that Woody Allen used as a location for his film *Purple Rose of Cairo*. Since the film was shot, fine restaurants, shops, boutiques, and a shopping arcade have opened. But this hamlet has maintained its original charm, and it's a lovely place to stop off on your way to Nyack (about fifteen minutes away by bus).

Seeing and Doing

Shop for antiques and collectibles, dine, and then walk over to the Landing, on the Hudson, where dozens of sailboats float on the river. If you want to be part of the nautical action, you can rent a rowboat at 124 Paradise Avenue at Main Street.

Eating There

There are several open-air cafes in the Landing, the shopping area along the Hudson, and on Main Street itself. Our favorite is the Turning Point, an old-fashioned restaurant that serves gourmet sandwiches—in warm weather you can sit on the wooden front porch.

Staying There

There are no hotels in Piermont, but it still makes for a fine day trip.

Easton, PA

... home of Crayola factory—
a treat for kids of all ages

DAY OR WEEKEND TRIP; KID-FRIENDLY

Getting There

The Transbridge bus (800-962 9135) at Port Authority, bound for Allentown, stops in Easton's town square at the Civil War memorial, which is surrounded by fountains and shops. The ride is about two hours long.

Being There: Then and Now

Easton was home to the Leni Lenape Indian Tribe when the first European settlers landed at Lechawitank, the Indian name for "place at the forks," the land between the Delaware and Lehigh Rivers. The town was founded in 1752 by William Penn's sons, Thomas and John Penn. On July 8, 1776, the citizens of Easton gathered in the town square for a public reading of the Declaration of Independence. Easton was one of only three cities in which the document was read aloud to the public that day.

Today Easton is home to historic museums, bright red trolleys, a mule barge along the canal, and the Binney &

Smith Crayola Factory. Thousands of families from all over the country visit the crayon factory throughout the year. Here, children can watch the crayons and markers being manufactured, then try them out.

Easton has recently emerged from a severe economic depression which spanned nearly two decades—it was rescued by the joint efforts of the municipality, the state, and the private sector, with Crayola as a principal investor. This restoration has become a model program for other American cities and towns.

Seeing and Doing

Your first stop is the Crayola Factory at 2 Rivers Landing where five million crayons are produced daily—enough to circle the globe four and a half times or make one giant crayon 100 feet taller than the Statue of Liberty. On their tour, kids are encouraged to let their imaginations take flight in a special room "just for daydreaming." Visit the Crayola Hall of Fame, which displays the sweater that Fred Rogers, of "Mr. Rogers' Neighborhood," wore on the show February 6, 1996, when he made the 100 billionth Crayola crayon at the factory. The Hall also honors Bingo, the world's only coloring dog. There is lots more to see and do during your visit to the factory. One of our favorite stops is the "Bright Idea Laboratory," where visitors can explore the science of color and light. (Some colorful history: Crayola founders, Mr. Binney and Mr. Smith, got their start painting tires black—they used to be white—and barns red.) Of course, there's a souvenir shop, and if the kids are hungry, there's a McDonalds right in the building.

A bright red hop-on-hop-off trolley waits outside the Crayola factory to carry you past a lovely riverside park, quaint old buildings, and the town's shops and restaurants. Your tour guide describes the highlights, and the trolley can drop you at any destination along the way—the entire town can be walked in about twenty minutes.

On Northampton Street is Tailwaggers and Treasure Alley, an unusual antique shop where vintage dolls, statuettes, cups, plates, trays, pillows, and jewelry all depict cats and dogs. Scotties are a favorite item, and when we were there, the proprietor's Scotty and Westie dozed in the shop window, as though they were part of the display. There are several other antiques shops along Northampton. Two blocks from Northampton is Easton's prettiest street, Spring Garden Street which is lined with gracious homes. Here, also are Reflections Gallery and the Spring Garden Street Gallery, two floors of exquisite treasures and a cafe with indoor and outdoor dining.

From Spring Garden, you can take the trolley to the Hugh Moore Historical Park and Museum and the *Josia White II* barge which is pulled by two mules along the Lehigh Canal. The park is home to the Locktenders House Museum which displays canal boat and Erie Lackawanna railroad paraphernalia. There are picnic tables in the park if you feel like packing a lunch.

Eating There

If you walk along Northampton Street, toward the Delaware River, you come upon Larry Holmes Drive, named after the boxing champion who grew up in Easton. Mr. Holmes has enhanced his hometown with a complex housing a health club, a boxing ring, a small shopping arcade, and a restaurant —all at 91 Larry Holmes Drive (610-258-5752).

Most of Easton's eateries are near the village square, adjacent to the Crayola factory. The Easton Sweet Shop, 251 Northampton Street, is an old-fashioned luncheonette, and Pearly Baker's Ale House, 11 Center Square, a Victorian pub, is one of the best-known restaurants in the area. Check out the lovely indoor-outdoor cafe, Tachie, at the Spring Garden Street Gallery.

We walked across the Free Bridge to Phillipsburg, New Jersey, another village of seventeenth- and eighteenth-century structures in the process of renovation. We liked watching the hip-booted fishermen as we sat on the wooden porch of the Union Street Café.

Staying There

Just a short block from the bus stop, and right down the road from the Crayola factory is the Best Western Easton Inn at 185 South 3rd Street (800-528-1234 or 610-253-9131), which has more than two hundred clean, modern rooms. A short taxi ride takes you to the Lafayette Inn, with antique-filled rooms and landscaped gardens, at 525 West Monroe Street (610-253-4500), one block from the campus of Lafayette College.

New Hope, PA

. . . arts, crafts, and a mule barge along the Delaware Canal

DAY OR WEEKEND TRIP; KID-FRIENDLY

Getting There

Take the Transbridge bus (800-962-9135) from Port Authority to Lambertville. From there, the center of New Hope is just a short walk over the bridge that crosses the Delaware River.

Being There: Then and Now

New Hope, Pennsylvania, is surely one of the most beautiful small towns in America. In the village, a waterfall gushes behind old stone buildings, and stunningly preserved homes from colonial times line the streets and lanes that twist through this historic hamlet. Mule-drawn barges glide along a sleepy canal, and the Delaware River flows along the village's grassy banks.

The people of New Hope played a significant role during the Revolutionary War. They aided the retreating Continental Army by taking them downriver to a neighboring town, where the army began the march on Trenton that was instrumental in defeating the British on December 26, 1776. New Hope prospered after the war and sent flaxseed oil, lumber, whiskey, and coal up and down the Delaware.

In the early 1900s, artists who were drawn by the beauty of the Bucks County countryside established an artist's colony in New Hope that became world renowned. The interior of one old grist mill has been transformed into the famous Bucks County Playhouse. Beginning in 1977, with financial assistance from the New Hope Historical Society and the borough government, Ann Nieson researched every structure over 100 years old. In 1985, 243 New Hope properties were accepted for inclusion on the National Register of Historic Places, and New Hope is now a tourist mecca that draws huge weekend crowds. But this is a town you have to experience—throngs or not—and there are tranquil places to be found along the river, or across the bridge in Lambertville, New Jersey (see page 93).

Seeing and Doing

As you take in the sights, stop at the original Ferry Tavern, the oldest building in New Hope, at the corner of South Main and Ferry Streets. The Beaumont House (1788), with its walled courtyard, is directly across the street. In 1784, Benjamin Parry built a fieldstone house in the center of town where five generations of his family lived. In 1966, the New Hope Historical Society purchased this house and restored it as a museum of decorative arts. The Parry Mansion is open to the public on Friday through Sunday, from May through October.

Particularly worth a visit is the Ney Museum on Mechanic Street. Ney, whose art is permanently exhibited in New York's Museum of Modern Art, left New Hope a huge body of work depicting the life of the town in the 1940s and 1950s.

When you long for a respite, walk down to the banks of the Delaware to the Delaware Canal Gardens, 24 riverside gardens bright with plantings and flowers. While lingering in the gardens, you can feed the geese that congregate along the water's edge at the sound of human voices. Just be prepared for a quick departure: They challenge you with honking and flapping when you run out of crumbs.

You can enjoy a cruise boat that trundles past New Hope, Lambertville, and other sites along the river, or walk a few blocks to the Mule Barge Landing on the canal for a mule-drawn boat ride.

New Hope has several live theaters, and local nightspots featuring cabaret, comedy, and music by internationally known performers. The Towpath House, located on Mechanic Street (215-862-3777), and the Bucks County Playhouse on Main St. (215-862-2041) both offer legitimate theater with Equity players.

If children are with you, take a ride on the old steam engine in the turreted train station at the top of Bridge Street. The New Hope & Ivyland Railroad, built in 1889, takes you to Lahaska and back, traveling through woodlands past several homes that were part of the Underground Railroad—a narrator points out the historical sites.

For more information about New Hope's artistic and historic highlights, call the New Hope Information Center at 215-862-5880, or drop by the Center at 1 West Mechanic Street (at the corner of Main St.).

Eating There

One of our favorite places to eat in New Hope is Canal House at 26-34A Mechanic Street, smack-dab on the canal, where you can dine in the garden in summer and on the enclosed deck in winter. A popular hangout for locals and visitors at almost any hour is Mothers, located on North Main Street (215-862-9384), open for breakfast, lunch, dinner, and late-night snacks. After you eat, you might want to take home a fresh-baked pie or cake from the restaurant bakery. Classic cuisine, served in a comfortable country dining room or on a spacious patio overlooking the Delaware, can be had for lunch or dinner at The Landing on 22 Main Street (215-862-5711).

Staying There

The New Hope Inn (36 West Mechanic Street, 888-272-2078) offers cable TV, room service, and air conditioning in country-style rooms that surround a sparkling, heated outdoor pool. The Wedgwood Inn (111 West Bridge Street, 215-862-2570) provides gracious accommodations and a sumptuous breakfast in three separate houses (one is the Aaron Burr House) furnished with Early American antiques.

Peddler's Village, PA

. . . shopping—colonial style, and a magical museum
of merry-go-rounds

DAY OR WEEKEND TRIP; KID-FRIENDLY

Getting There

Peddler's Village is in an area of Bucks County called Lahaska. Transbridge buses (800-962-9135) leave Port Authority several times a day to make the two-hour trip (the bus' ultimate destination is Doylestown). The bus stop is right up the road from the Golden Plough Inn; ask the driver to let you off in front.

Being There: Then and Now

Imagine yourself in an English country village, say, a charming hamlet in the Lake District—where you're doing some serious American shopping. But Earl Hart Lamison was actually inspired by Carmel, California, when he opened The Golden Plough Inn and the Peddler's Village shopping complex on property that formerly housed the Hen Town chicken farm. Colonial Americana is the architectural style of these picturesque shops of brick, clapboard and stone featuring delightful, many-paned, mullioned windows.

The Village consists of over seventy specialty shops and six restaurants, landscaped with little arched bridges, tiny waterfalls, beguiling gardens, and winding brick paths. All this charm is set in the rolling countryside of gorgeous Bucks County. Just in case you start experiencing charm overload, down the road is the Penn's Purchase outlet center, a cluster of stores selling top brand names at discount prices.

Seeing and Doing

Prepare for a shopping and eating spree. The shops sell everything from country crafts, unique boutique clothing, decorative arts, jewelry, and collectibles to all varieties of gourmet foods. There are no chain stores here.

Peddler's Village presents continuous special events and exhibits that vary with the season, many of them wonderful to share with children. For instance, there's a teddy bear picnic with teddy bear floats, Dixieland music, and an old-fashioned backyard circus; in September is the scarecrow festival and December brings a Christmas festival featuring a national gingerbread house contest. In the spring, there are Amish quilt displays, strawberry festivals, and art fairs. A most exciting year-round spot in Peddler's Village is the Carousel World Museum, where you can take a ride on a colorful antique carousel. For information about lodging, fairs, and activities, call 215-794-4000.

Eating There

Peddler's Village has about half a dozen pubs and restaurants. The Spitted Hog, housed off the lobby of the Golden Plough, is great for a country breakfast or lunch. Jenny's

Restaurant just across the road, serves scrumptious food for lunch and dinner in a colorful colonial atmosphere, enhanced by beautiful stained-glass windows.

The most popular restaurant is the Cock and Bull, a multilevel eatery that welcomes you into a charming "common room" with a great stone hearth (and colonial cooking demonstrations in winter). Also worth checking out is the Peddler's Pub, a funky tavern that features "Murder Mystery" interactive theater on Friday and Saturday evenings from September through December.

Staying There

The Golden Plough Inn is the only place to stay in Peddler's Village. This lovely inn has hideaway rooms scattered in surprising places all around the village (several directly above the antique carousel). In every room is a fridge containing a split of complimentary champagne, along with juices and sodas, a basket of snacks, and a gracious letter of welcome from your host, Mr. Jamison.

Sharing with friends makes even the loveliest rooms very affordable. Ask for one of the luxurious suites with bubbling Jacuzzi, gas fireplace, and a four-poster bed (an additional bed comes with the room). Less expensive rooms can be found over the Cock and Bull, but expect a bit of music and chatter.

During our stay in Peddler's Village, we felt like princesses. Our room, just above the carousel museum, had a king-size canopy bed and a double sleighbed in the corner. Our fireplace was glowing, as we toasted our host with a glass of champagne after our Murder Mystery Escapade dinner.

Philadelphia, PA

. . . Society Hill; Old City; Independence Park

DAY OR WEEKEND TRIP; KID-FRIENDLY

Getting There

Amtrak trains (800-872-7245) leave about every hour from Penn Station to Philadelphia's 30th Street Station. Greyhound (800-231-2222) and Peter Pan (800-343-9999) leave Port Authority several times a day for Philadelphia. A cab ride from the station takes only a few minutes to the attractions, inns, and hotels in the historic areas we describe.

Being There: Then and Now

America's fifth largest city and the nation's first capital, Philadelphia is bustling, historic, and charming—"the town that loves you back"—and it's only about two hours from New York. You can spend several days exploring, museum-hopping, antiquing, nightclubbing, and boat riding, or do a little of each on a weekend or even during a day trip. Our description here focuses on a weekend visit to Independence National Historic Park, Old City, Society Hill, and Penn's Landing.

Independence National Historic Park encompasses most of Philadelphia's famous historic sites, including the Liberty Bell, Independence Hall, and Franklin Court—where you can see Ben Franklin's many inventions. Old City is a burgeoning artists' district adjacent to Penn's Landing where water taxis will ferry you across the river to the Camden Aquarium. Society Hill, near Independence Hall, is a beautiful historic and antiquing area.

If you have an extra day to spend, you might enjoy a guided tour to the Brandywine River Valley and an afternoon at Longwood Gardens.

Seeing and Doing

Take a taxi from the train or bus stations down to Old City, once a manufacturing section with industrial lofts and factories. Now, more than forty art galleries and showrooms are tucked into old buildings along timeworn cobblestone streets You can walk through Old City from its border at Front Street up Chestnut Street to Sixth Street, site of Independence National Historic Park and the Liberty Bell. Walk a block to Fifth Street, and park rangers will guide you to Independence Hall's Assembly Room, where the Declaration of Independence and the Constitution were signed. The Visitor's Center in the park provides tours and maps to all colonial and federal landmarks. For more information call 215-636-3300.

Society Hill: Walk across Independence Park to Walnut Street where you'll find a cluster of pristine red-brick colonial homes, some in small courtyards, lined along Philadelphia's narrow two-lane main streets. You can reminisce about the times when Thomas Jefferson and Ben Franklin strolled these very streets, and Betsy Ross designed America's first flag. You can hire a horse-drawn carriage at Independence Historical Park at Fifth and Chestnut for a relaxing look at the historic district. A courtesy van (923-8516) can pick you up from anywhere in the city and deliver you here. On Second Street, off Walnut, is Headhouse Square, cobblestone streets surrounded by restaurants and shops, with an open-air marketplace every summer weekend in the center. Serene and lovely Pine Street, known as Antique Row, runs from the Square and sells quilts, wicker furnishings, and other Americana. Intriguing South Street, just two blocks away, with its jumble of clothing and antiques shops and cafes, is always active and fun.

Walk back down South Street to Penn's Landing on the Delaware River waterfront. You can ferry over to the Camden Aquarium (in New Jersey) from here. Penn's Landing also offers a look at a tall ship, a submarine tour, boat rides, entertainment, and festivals.

We would be remiss if we didn't mention the bright red-and-green trolley that can take you to Philadelphia's marvelous sights from the mansions of Fairmount Park (ten times the size of Central Park), along the Schuylkill River where crews row, to the Reading Terminal Market, an enormous indoor farmer's market with food stalls of cuisines from all over the world. This is a truly wonderful place to go if you have extended time.

You can also take a day tour of the Brandywine River Valley. A bus run by Brandywine Tours (610-358-5445) picks you up at your hotel and drives you through the picturesque, pastoral countryside made famous by Andrew Wyeth. The bus takes you to the Brandywine Museum which is housed in a converted Civil War grist mill. This glass-enclosed structure has unobstructed views of winding streams, gently rolling hills, and sun-dappled meadows, a perfect backdrop for its exhibit of Wyeth paintings. The afternoon of the tour is spent at Longwood Gardens, once the home of a DuPont, now a thousand-acre wonderland of lush lawns and flower gardens. Since it's not possible to get to the Brandywine Valley in Delaware from New York City without a car, we were particularly excited to discover this tour from Philadelphia.

Eating There

One of our favorite restaurants is City Tavern on Second Street. Lace-capped waitresses serve Early American cuisine in an old, recently restored colonial inn, with wide plank floors, pine tables, and stone hearths decorated with pewter plates and mugs. We love the warm and intimate ambiance, and highly recommend it for maintaining a colonial-Philadelphia frame of mind.

Ristorante Panorama, at Penn's View Inn (at Front and Market Streets) in Old City, is a beautiful spot that feels like a garden in Italy. The restaurant's justly famous wine bar offers one hundred and twenty different wines by the glass, and the bartender is quite knowledgeable. We enjoyed sampling the "Panoramic Flight," one-ounce glasses of five different international wines.

What's a trip to Philadelphia without Bookbinders? World-famous for its seafood, it is in the Society Hill district on Second Street and Walnut, right across from City Tavern. In Philadelphia you must also have a cheese-steak sandwich.

Stand in line at Jim's Steaks at Fourth and South Streets, and decide whether to have yours with (onions) or without.

Staying There

The Penn's View Inn, a historic landmark at Front and Market Streets (215-922-7600), is located in Old City within a stone's throw of all the special places we love to visit. Its twenty-eight guest rooms are decorated with distinctive Old World charm. For a luxurious visit, request a room with a Jacuzzi and fireplace. A generous continental breakfast buffet is included, and weekend packages are available.

The Independence Park Inn, at 235 Chestnut Street (215-922-4443), is a lovely small hotel, adjacent to Philadelphia's historic square mile. This Best Western Hotel offers guest rooms with high ceilings, a complimentary breakfast in a glass-enclosed courtyard, and a grand lobby with a roaring fireplace.

Travel Notes

_____

_____

_____

_____

_____

_____

_____

_____

_____

_____

_____

_____

_____

_____

_____

_____

_____

_____

_____

_____

_____

_____

_____

Two
and a
Half
Hours

Essex, CT

. . . one of the prettiest villages in America

WEEKEND TRIP

Getting There

Take an Amtrak train (800-USA-RAIL) from Penn Station to Old Saybrook. From there, call Essex Taxi (767-7433) to pick you up at the station and take you to the Griswold Inn. While you wait, you can browse in the adjoining antiques emporium or sip a soda at the small cafe.

Being There: Then and Now

The town of Essex was established in 1654, after the English won the area in battle from the Dutch. Its proximity to the river and its shipbuilding prowess soon made seaborne commerce central to the economy of Essex. Homes were built with widow's walks where wives could watch for the approach of their husbands' ships returning from long stretches at sea. During the Revolutionary War, the 24-gun *Oliver Cromwell*, the first ship of the Continental Navy, was built in Essex.

Today wandering through Essex conjures up peaceful

feelings. This delightful village has been called "one of the prettiest in America" and was named number one in the 1996 publication of *The 100 Best Small Towns in America* by Norman Crampton. Colonial shuttered saltboxes, grand sprawling stone houses, and a smattering of New England churches are clustered on Main and Pratt Streets. Many specialty shops (some surrounded by gardens) line both sides of the road with little walks leading to a tiny mews.

Seeing and Doing

Visit the Connecticut Museum (860-767-8269) at the end of Main Street at Steamboat Dock, where you can trace the history of the Connecticut River, the longest river in the state, once called "the great river" by the English. The museum is housed in a Victorian warehouse where spices and oils imported from the West Indies were stored. On display is a permanent exhibit of ship models, navigational, and ship-building tools, and paintings, some of which depict the burning of the ships at Essex during the War of 1812. Museum hours are Tuesday through Sunday, 10 A.M. to 5 P.M., year round.

If you'd like to bicycle around the town, you can rent a single or tandem bike at Main Street's Bike Rentals (to reserve a tandem ahead of time, call 860-767-7376). In 1971 a group of townspeople dedicated to preserving railroad history formed the Valley Railroad Company, which now offers old-fashioned steam train rides. The steam train, built in the early 1920s, puffs and chugs and whistles, flashing its lights and ringing its bells along a century-old route, year round. It can take you to the paddlewheel boat that carries passengers past the Gillette Castle, home of the Goodspeed Opera Company, on the other side of the river.

To walk to the Valley Railroad train station, turn up Main Street, away from the river, take a left on South Main, and turn right when you reach West Avenue. Walk along West until you get to Route 154. At your right, are signs for the Valley Railroad Steam Engine Company. The walk takes about a half hour, but if you're not in a hiking frame of mind or body, call Essex Taxi (767-7433) for a ride. There's also a stationary dining car where you can buy sandwiches and drinks to take on the ride, and an irresistible gift shop filled with delightful railroad paraphernalia. We bought a large steam diesel alarm clock that wakes you to clangs, whistles, and chugs.

Eating There

A complimentary continental breakfast is served in the library at the Griswold Inn to all guests from 7 to 10 A.M. every day. On Sundays, the "Gris" offers its traditional Hunt Breakfast, begun by the British when they occupied the inn during the War of 1812. Children 6 and under eat free of charge. Unlimited quantities of fresh fruits, chicken, fish, eggs, soufflés, and roasted meats are served from 11 A.M. to 2:30 P.M.

The Griswold Tap Room was built in 1734 as a one-room schoolhouse. In the center is a large black potbellied stove, purchased from the Goodspeed Opera House at the turn of the century. To add extra warmth, a fire crackles in a woodburning fireplace. There's even an antique popcorn machine continuously spilling out hot popcorn as you drink, eat, and enjoy the evening's entertainment that ranges from ragtime and Dixieland jazz to old sea chanties (depending on the night of the week).

Dine in the Griswold's Covered Bridge Room, built from aged timber rescued from an old bridge. It features an impressive collection of Currier and Ives steamboat prints.

Staying There

The historic Griswold Inn (860-767-1776), which first opened to the public in 1776, is the place to stay in Essex. During the War of 1812, the British Commonwealth made the Griswold its base of operations in the Connecticut Valley. The Tap Room was moved to the main inn in the late eighteenth century by a team of oxen rolling it on logs down Main Street. The inn owns and displays several outstanding collections, including rifles and handguns dating back to the fifteenth century, and a group of marine oil paintings. Guest rooms at the "Gris" are charmingly decorated with reproduction colonial wallpaper, colorful hooked rugs, and high brass beds, but the private baths, telephones, and television sets (tastefully disguised) are decidedly modern.

Hartford, CT

. . . a surprisingly cheery winter holiday destination

WEEKEND TRIP; KID-FRIENDLY

Getting There

The Amtrak train (800-USA-RAIL) at Penn Station will take you to Hartford in two and a half hours. Greyhound (800-231-2222) and Peter Pan buses (800-343-9999) leave for Hartford from Port Authority. The trip takes a little more than two and a half hours.

Being There: Then and Now

It was Wednesday afternoon, the day before Thanksgiving, and everybody we knew was going away for the holiday weekend. Our parents lived in Florida, our almost adult children were "booked" at friends' houses for the weekend, and we were suddenly struck with the seemingly stark reality that, not having planned ahead for this touted American holiday, we had nowhere to go.

"Hartford?" our friends asked. "It's the insurance capital of the country," they reminded us (as if we weren't already familiar with that particular distinction), "you might as well stay in Manhattan!" Of course, *they* were all on their way to family celebrations at other peoples' homes or in quaint New England inns. We called a few of those places, but they were all solidly booked for the four-day weekend.

We remembered the previous Sunday's *Times*. The Sheraton Hotel in Hartford, it said, offered room, bath, and morning brunch for a special "holiday" discount rate—and we'd never been to Hartford. So we made a reservation for the day after Thanksgiving.

It turned out to be a perfect choice. Less than a five-minute walk from the train station, the Sheraton's twenty-two-story building towered over the Hartford streetscape. The hotel provided a full health club with Olympic-size pool, VCRs on request, and coffee in every room.

On the eve of Hartford's traditional three-week Festival of Lights we were welcomed by seasonally costumed characters singing carols. After checking in, we lunched at a pub overlooking Church Street—the view of cobblestones, gas lamps, chestnut vendors, ladies wrapped in velvet capes and wide crinolined skirts, and carolers made us feel as if we were in London at the time of David Copperfield and Oliver Twist.

At 4 P.M. we met on the front steps of the hotel with a group of colorful, Victorian-clad entertainers and followed them along the cobblestones of Pratt Street, our parade expanding with every few steps we took, until our numbers had swelled to hundreds when we reached the Statehouse (the oldest in America) at Constitution Plaza. There were couples with dogs and clusters of children, balloons, and streamers floating above our heads, vendors selling roasted chestnuts, hot cider, and tarts.

There were more Christmas carols, a welcome from

the mayor, and finally the clattering noises above us in the darkening skies where a helicopter circled. To the cheering of crowds, Santa, attached to a bright red-and-white parachute, descended right onto the plaza. Then the lights—thousands of them—broke the darkness into a glittering streetscape and everybody (even us) cheered. It was a perfect place to be. The Hartford Festival of Lights takes place every year on the day after Thanksgiving.

Seeing and Doing

Most of the attractions are within walking distance of the railroad station. The visitor's center in the Old State House provides maps and booklets for a self-guided walking tour. You can also pick up an audiocassette that literally talks you though the city's highlights and history.

The Old State House, a handsome federal-style building built in 1796, was saved from demolition by Hartford's concerned citizens. It's a beautifully preserved landmark. All of the original architectural details of the rooms which housed the courtroom and state and house chambers have been lovingly restored. Believe it or not, the Colt Revolver that we generally associate with the Wild West was actually invented in Hartford in 1836 by Hartford native Sam Colt. Colt's collection of firearms, including a Wyatt Earp six-shooter and M2 and M3 aircraft guns, are housed in the Museum of Connecticut History, at 231 Capital Avenue (203-566-3056). While there, look for the exhibits of early American watches and clocks, designed and manufactured by Connecticut clockmakers. Take note: this museum is open only in the morning.

America's first free public art museum, the Wadsworth Athenaeum, located at 600 Main Street, was established in 1842. We enjoyed strolling through the Wadsworth on a Sunday morning, viewing fine paintings and furnishings by American artists. The museum cafe serves a delectable Sunday brunch.

Skyscrapers dominate the downtown skyline, but Hartford boasts gracious historic homes and landmark buildings too. Just a short taxi ride from the center of the city is Nook Farm (77 Forest Street, off Farmington Avenue), the restoration of a Victorian artists' colony settled in the late 1800s. Important writers and celebrities have lived in Hartford, including Harriet Beecher Stowe, author of *Uncle Tom's Cabin*, and Samuel Clemens (better known as Mark Twain). Twain's house is painted "turkey" red, and its south façade is modeled after a Mississippi River steamboat. His telephone, which he reputedly despised and ignored, is located in a closet. The windows in the third-floor study, where he wrote *Tom Sawyer* and *Huckleberry Finn*, are etched with depictions of his great passions in life—smoking, drinking, and billiards.

Our afternoon treat was an amble through Bushnell Park, where we fixed our gaze on the brilliant gold dome of the state capitol. This is Hartford's most magnificent outdoor work of art. One-hour tours of the building are conducted throughout the year (860-240-0222 for information). For more information, call the Convention and Visitors Bureau at 860-674-1035.

Eating There

Many pubs and restaurants are close to the station. Gaetino's (860-249-8624), located in the Civic Center, adjacent to the Sheraton Hotel, serves excellent, moderately priced Italian cuisine. This glass-enclosed restaurant is a colorful and festive place. Chuck's Steakhouse, also at the Civic Center (860-241-9100), is a cozy eatery filled with bamboo tables and chairs. The Sheraton has two comfortable and lively places for casual fare: Huckleberry's and Finn's Sports Bar.

Staying There

There are a number of accommodations in downtown Hartford, and most offer weekend packages. We found the Sheraton Hartford (860-728-5151) a hospitable and convenient place to stay. When you leave the bus/train station, walk up Church Street, turn at Pratt Street, and enter the hotel at Pratt and Trumble Streets. The hotel is part of the Civic Center, a huge complex with a brightly lit indoor shopping mall and many restaurants. Its glass-enclosed catwalks overlook the bustling street below.

If you prefer smaller, more intimate accommodations, we recommend the Goodwin Hotel (860-246-7500), just across the street from the Sheraton at One Haynes Street—a charming historic building. The Goodwin features sleigh beds and country décor.

*   *   *

Our trip to Hartford was one of the most pleasurable of all—and we are still warmed by the memories.

Southbury, CT

. . . a great resort for the whole family

WEEKEND TRIP; KID-FRIENDLY

Getting There

Bonanza buses (800-556-3815) leave from Port Authority to Southbury approximately every two hours. Your destination is the Heritage Inn. When you make reservations (203-264-8200 or 800-932-3466) you can arrange to be picked up from the station.

Seeing and Doing

During the fall and winter months, Mom, you can relax in the Overlook Lounge (that means "overlooking the kids") near a blazing hearth while family and friends swim in an indoor pool and stretch out in a bubbling Jacuzzi. The family can play water volleyball, Ping-Pong, and racquetball, and of course if you're inspired, you can even join them. If you don't want to sweat or get wet, you can merely glance over as they engage in darts, billiards, board games, or cards in the game room where a fire will keep you nice and toasty (we won't mention the large-screen TV; after all, this is a weekend for doing).

If it's spring or summer, you can all be outside swimming, playing tennis, biking along wooded trails, trout fishing, jogging, playing a game of horseshoes or croquet, or even golfing (there are nine- and eighteen-hole PGA rated courses). There's even more, from horseback riding to hot-air ballooning to skiing (downhill and cross-country) to sleigh rides to horse-drawn hayrides or carriage rides, and last, but certainly not least, a quaint indoor shopping arcade featuring crafts, clothing, and little treasures for the home.

Staying There (and Eating There):

A rambling lodge surrounded by wooded trails, Heritage Inn has 163 newly decorated guest rooms with New England–style décor. There are two restaurants on the premises. Timbers on the Green, the Inn's dining room, and Splash, an art deco bistro that serves up food and entertainment. Call for information (800-932-3466) about package deals and weekend rates.

Yes, you could spend a week here during any season and, except for golf fees, massage services, food, and beverage costs, all the activities are free.

Wethersfield, CT

... classic, early-American town with

seventeenth-century homes

WEEKEND TRIP; KID-FRIENDLY

Getting There

Take the Amtrak train (800-USA-RAIL) to Hartford from Penn Station. The trip takes about three hours, so it's best to plan an overnight stay. When you call to make reservations (at least two weeks ahead of time for the only lodging establishment in town, The Chester Bulkley House Bed and Breakfast Inn), tell innkeepers Frank and Sophie Bottaro your time of arrival—they will have you picked up at the Hartford Station for a nominal fee ($5.00 each way).

Being There: Then and Now

Imagine a village where a hundred and fifty homes are over 125 years old—and in perfect condition. Established in 1634 and listed on the National Register of Historic Places, Wethersfield is the oldest town in Connecticut. In the mid-1600s, Wethersfield's harbor (now the Cove) became the commerce center for the Connecticut River Valley. Exports—including farm animals, flax seed, and the red onions for which Wethersfield was known—left for places as far away as the West Indies on ships built and manned by Wethersfield seamen.

Swept up in the witchcraft hysteria that spread through the colonies in the 1600s, Wethersfield's first witch execution took place in 1648. The town is the setting of the award-winning children's book, *The Witch of Blackbird Pond.*

With its lengthy main street and little side roads, Wethersfield is an ideal walking town.

Seeing and Doing

So, on to those wonderful early American structures. Some stand alone as museums to be explored; others house fine shops, a church, and a tiny synagogue. The rest are private residences. Wethersfield citizens have lived in them continuously since the 1600s.

Your first stop should be the Keeney Memorial Cultural Center at 200 Main Street (860-529-7656, open Tuesday–Saturday, 10 A.M. to 4 P.M.). Constructed as a school in 1893, this building was restored by the Wethersfield Historical Society. You can pick up maps and brochures and learn all about this vintage community from a variety of exhibits. And you can learn a great deal about the people who established this town by taking one of the burial-ground tours offered throughout the year.

Most of the old buildings are on Main Street between Center and Church Streets, including the Wethersfield Fire Department. Chartered in 1803, this is the oldest volunteer fire department in continuous existence in the United States. Next door is the 1788 Isaac Stevens House. The house remained in the Stevens family until 1957, when it was acquired by the Connecticut division of the National Society of the Colonial Dames. The Silas Deane House was built in 1766 by an attorney who, as a member of the First Continental Congress, was sent to Paris in 1776, to negotiate with the French government for arms and supplies for the Revolutionary forces.

Main Street has many antique shops and galleries. We love the Red Barn Christmas shop, a festive place. Among Wethersfield's annual civic celebrations is a May weekend featuring reenactments of a Revolutionary War encampment and the signing of important treaties. Participants dress in period costumes, a riverboat whisks you along the Connecticut River, and a trolley takes you to all the village highlights.

Eating There

Amici's, a new and very popular Italian restaurant on Main Street, is currently the only place to get a full-course dinner. Village Pizza and Sweet Gatherings both serve a lunch menu. When you have breakfast at the inn, the Bottaros will be glad to tell you about any new restaurants that have opened.

Staying There

The Chester Bulkley House (860-563-4236), the only inn in town, is a Greek Revival home which has been beautifully restored. The guestrooms have antique period furnishings and are fresh, bright, very pretty—and air-conditioned. A lavish breakfast is served each morning. The patio out back, where guests are welcome, is surrounded by an English summer garden of foxgloves and delphiniums.

Atlantic City, NJ

... not for gamblers only

DAY OR WEEKEND TRIP

Getting There

Port Authority (212-564-8484) has bus service to Atlantic
City via New Jersey Transit (201-212-8484) or Academy
Lines (212-971-9054). Buses leave every hour on the hour
and the trip takes two and one-half hours. Ten dollars worth
of quarters are given to each traveler on board compliments
of the casinos. Try not to spend it all on the slot machines.
Academy buses also make pick-ups at a number of other
Manhattan locations (call 212-971-9054 for more information). If you prefer train travel, you can take Amtrak (800-
872-7245) from Penn Station to Atlantic City.

Being There: Then and Now

Atlantic City is about more than just "hitting the casinos."
It's also about the boardwalk which offers a long good-for-
spring stroll past wrought-iron gas lamps and shops selling
tchotchkes and saltwater taffy. You can be pushed along in an
oversize white wicker pram as you could long ago, when
Atlantic City was pure Americana and became the site for

the Miss America Pageant. Even in winter, the boardwalk bustles with activity—you can't help but hear the sounds of unfamiliar languages spoken by visitors from all over the world. If the street names sound familiar, that's because this is the town that inspired the board game Monopoly.

Seeing and Doing

If gambling isn't your cup of tea, just wandering along the lively promenade of glittering high-rise casino hotels (each with a different theme) is a feast for the ears and eyes, with live entertainment often spilling out to the corridors and lobbies. Look for the bejeweled marble elephants that guard the swirling stone stairways to Trump's Taj Mahal. Follow the ruby-red carpeting into the Taj to the blasting brilliance of the casino halls.

Huge alabaster statues beckon you into the dramatic columned halls of Caesar's Palace, where you are surrounded by staff in togas and tunics bearing trays of drinks, handing out chips, and guiding you to the blackjack tables.

Across the boardwalk from Caesar's looks to be a huge ocean liner—it is really a shopping arcade. Once known as the Million Dollar Pier, the original structure dates back to 1906 and currently houses an indoor mall, The Shops on Ocean One, with more than 100 boutiques and 25 eateries.

Eating There

You never go hungry in Atlantic City, and the prices are astonishingly low. You can find examples of almost every cuisine in the casino hotels along the boardwalk. Each one has several eating spots. We particularly like The Irish Pub, a turn-of-the-century tavern just a few steps in from the boardwalk at New York Avenue. Its walls are covered with photos of boxing champions of the forties and fifties and you can have a good-sized ham or turkey sandwich, a mug of draft beer, and a cup of soup for about $2.99.

Staying There

Call AmeriRoom Reservations (800-888-5825) for a list of accommodations, or call Accommodations Express (800-444-7666) to inquire about lodging. During the off-season days of fall and winter, many of the lavish boardwalk hotels offer rooms at moderate prices, enabling you to spend more in their downstairs casinos.

We stayed at the Atlantic Palace (800-527-8483), on New York Avenue and the Boardwalk. The rooms are large and well furnished. Ask for a high floor, overlooking the ocean—the B line is excellent. In addition to a queen-size bed with upholstered headboard, we had two pull-out couches, a four-chair dining set, and a tiny kitchen with a microwave. If you don't want to venture outside and face the evening winds, you can order in pizza or Chinese food. For us the most exciting feature of this hotel is the pink Jacuzzi in each bathroom, tucked away behind a gauze-curtained window. When you pull back the curtains, you've hit the jackpot—the most dazzling views of the sky and lights are yours to behold.

Omega Institute

RHINEBECK, NEW YORK

. . . a sleepaway camp for adults

WEEKEND TRIP

Getting There

Omega operates a special charter bus (800-944-1001) that picks up and returns participants to the Penn Station area. Alternatively, you can take a Shortline bus (800-631-8405) from Port Authority to the Beekman Arms Hotel in Rhinebeck or an Amtrak train (800-USA-RAIL) from Penn Station to Rhinecliff. An Omega shuttle van will pick you up from either station. The 800 number above will provide you with schedule and price information for all the travel choices.

Being There: Then and Now

Omega is a unique learning center where you can explore and realize your deepest self, special talents, and capacity for happiness and celebration. It's an exhilarating experience shared with remarkable people from all over the world of varying professions, talents, and ages. You can bring your kids along, too. There's a program for children ages 4-12 during workshop hours. And you'll probably want to return summer after summer after summer. We do.

When you arrive at Omega, once a children's camp, you may be enveloped with the same warm glow you felt as a youngster embarking on a new adventure. You won't find color wars or have to wake to reveille flag raising; but you might find workshops in African drumming and dancing presided over by Baba Olatunji; fiction and poetry writing seminars led by Marge Piercy, Robert Bly, or Sharon Olds; or acting and storytelling sessions with Spalding Gray. You may get to make music with renowned cellist David Darling, Rosanne Cash, Bobby McFerrin, or Philip Glass; dance with Gabrielle Roth; discover your healing powers and spirituality with Stephen Levine and Deepak Chopra or embark on a week-long retreat with Buddhist Zen Master and Poet Thich Nhat Hanh.

You can sculpt statues, make pottery, draw from the left side of your brain, paint, or shoot, develop, and print photographs; all under the direction of world-renowned teachers who lead, prod, and inspire you to find your own special creative and spiritual self. Each workshop ends with an exhibition or performance that grows from the unique collaboration of minds and spirits.

Seeing and Doing

In addition to the two hundred and fifty workshops, there are daily yoga, tai chi, meditation, dance, and exercise classes. Sample sessions allow you to experience what various faculty members and programs have to offer. Evening activities include films, dances, musical performances, and late-night gatherings at the cafe.

The Wellness Center offers massage, bodywork, nutritional counseling, and saunas. If you're in a shopping mood, clothing, jewelry, international handicrafts, books, CDs, and tapes by Omega faculty are for sale. A tape shop can provide you with audiotapes of the workshop you just attended within hours of its completion. A cafe with indoor booths and umbrella-shaded outdoor tables sells sandwiches, salads, pasta dishes, ice cream, juices, teas, and home-baked goods every evening until 11 P.M. It's a popular hangout for just getting together and talking or singing—and there are always a couple of guitarists to oblige with accompaniment. Just walking along the wooded trails, swinging in a hammock under the trees, playing volleyball or tennis, canoeing, swimming, or lazing down by the lake are all wonderful things to do here.

For a complete catalog of courses, housing options, and travel information, call 800-862-8890 or 800-944-1001.

Eating There

Meals are served three times a day in a hilltop dining hall with many windows that look over the campus. Food is abundant, tasty, and mostly vegetarian (many of the fruits and vegetables are grown in Omega's own organic gardens), served buffet style, with second and third helpings for the taking. You can carry your tray out to the wide terrace porch that forms a huge half circle around the building, go down the steps to the picnic tables, or spread a picnic cloth on the lawn.

Dining is always a lively experience where people share their stories and current workshop experiences and discuss the evening entertainment programs they plan to attend.

Staying There

There are cabins with private or a shared bath, dormitories, in which each sleeping space is made private by partitions, and campsites (bring your own tenting gear)—with nearby bathhouses—along the lakefront or up in the hills.

Rhinebeck, NY

... home of America's oldest inn

DAY OR WEEKEND TRIP

Getting There

Shortline buses (800-631-8405) leave Port Authority for Rhinebeck twice a day and stop in front of the Beekman Arms Hotel. The trip takes about two hours. Amtrak trains (800-872-7245) leave Penn Station for Rhinecliff station several times a day. The train trip is an hour and forty minutes, but you'll have to take a short taxi ride from Rhinecliff to Rhinebeck. (Cabs are generally available at the station.) Although train tickets are more expensive, the beautiful train ride along the Hudson is worth it.

Being There: Then and Now

In 1715, thirty-five families fleeing persecution in the Rhine Valley settled in this mid–Hudson valley area as tenant farmers. They prospered, and Rhinebeck became known as the "breadbasket of New York City."

A former stagecoach stop for weary travelers en route from Albany to New York City, Rhinebeck was home to Traphagen's Tavern, now the Beekman Arms Hotel. Built two and a half centuries ago, the inn provided bed and board for travelers, and shelter for town residents against Indian attack. During the Revolutionary War, General Washington watched his troops drilling in a square from a corner window, and waited for his couriers to bring news from the battle-front; and the entire village population sought refuge at the inn following word of a possible British attack. Distinguished guests of the inn include Aaron Burr, Benedict Arnold, Alexander Hamilton, and Franklin Delano Roosevelt, who used to wind up his political campaigns on the hotel's front porch.

Seeing and Doing

The Beekman Arms Antique Barn, where more than thirty dealers sell an assortment of country collectibles and antiques, is located directly behind the main inn. There are also a number of stylish clothing and housewares shops, bookstores, and jewelry and art galleries to visit in the village. In addition, Rhinebeck hosts a variety of crafts, antiques, and horse shows throughout the year.

Eating There

An American Place Country Restaurant, located in the Beekman Arms, received an excellent rating by the *New York Times,* and serves prime rib, duck, chicken, and other regional specialties. Make a reservation for the sunny indoor garden or for the dark wood-paneled Colonial Tap Room, the center of the original inn. Also be sure to visit Schemmy's, an old-fashioned luncheonette/diner, and don't miss the London broil at Foster's.

Staying There

The Beekman Arms (4 Mill Street, on Route 9, 914-876-7077) is located in the center of the village of Rhinebeck. The oldest inn in America, it has fifty-nine guestrooms and suites, many with working fireplaces, and there's often a complimentary decanter of sherry. Down the street from the inn is the Delamater House (914-876-7080), an early example of American Capsite Gothic architecture. It was designed by one of America's first architects, Andrew Jackson Davis, and built in 1844. The parlor has a fireplace and wicker furniture. There is an adjoining courtyard and a cluster of six guesthouses, each with spacious accommodations and woodburning fireplaces.

Sag Harbor, NY

. . . charming nineteenth-century whaling village

DAY OR WEEKEND TRIP

Getting There

Take the Hampton Jitney (800-936-0449/0440) to Sag Harbor. It departs four times a day, and picks up passengers at several places in Manhattan. When you call for a reservation, ask for their current schedule, prices, and pick-up points. On a light-traffic day travel time is about two and a half hours. Comfortable seating, a restroom, and free beverages and snacks all make the busride quite pleasant.

Being There: Then and Now

Sag Harbor, on Gardiner's Bay at the east end of Long Island, was such a bustling port and shipbuilding center that George Washington declared it an official United States port of entry in 1789. It later became a major whaling port.

Now a National Historic District, Sag Harbor is one of the prettiest villages we visited. Restaurants, boutiques, and collectible shops are plentiful in the beautiful nineteenth-century buildings lining Main Street. We love the Variety Five-and-Dime Store, with its bright red and yellow awning shaded by gnarled old trees. Antique shops in tiny covered shacks, weathered barns, and cobbled mews are tucked away on the side streets.

Seeing and Doing

After poking through shops and lunching on fresh shrimp at a bayside restaurant, we visited the Sag Harbor Whaling and Historical Museum at Main and Garden Streets, then crossed the street to the John Tremaine Library with its 60-foot dome. Later, we walked up the road to the famous Whaler's Church at East Union Street which had its 187-foot steeple destroyed in the hurricane of 1938.

The Whaling Museum—a handsome, white-columned building, built in 1845 as a home for Captain Benjamin Hunting—features displays of ship models, tools, documents, artifacts, fashions, and even toys of the times. Sag Harbor's whaling days ended in the 1850s when the Gold Rush began, and the working people left for the hills.

Our next destination was the Custom House, right across from the Whaling Museum. This wonderful shingled 1789 building, with a wide brick path leading to the front door, housed the first post office on Long Island. Furnishings and documents of the time are on display.

If you stay the entire weekend, consider taking a cruise of the Peconic and Gardiner's Bay aboard the American Beauty, a 45-foot sightseeing boat. On the 90-minute sail you pass tranquil coves and Gardiner's Island. This thousand-acre island of woodlands and meadows is home to a bird and wildlife sanctuary where one of the largest populations of osprey in the Northeast nest on specially built platforms and in tall trees.

In fine weather, you might want to rent a bike on Main Street down by the wharf and ride to the public beach.

If you love the town's charming old buildings, you can purchase a tiny replica of one at the Hadley Studio, at 97 Main Street. Mr. Hadley and his "elves" miniaturize historically important buildings of the area, and, as he puts it, "cut the Hamptons down to size." His gift shop/studio is a wonderful place for browsing.

Eating There

There are several restaurants along Main Street, leading down to the waterfront. We chose a weathered shack, part of Malloy's Dockside Restaurant, with picnic tables on the side, for a fresh seafood lunch. At dinner, we had salad and appetizers at Spinnaker's on Main Street, a cozy place with high booths and a pretty garden for outdoor dining, just a few steps from the Jitney stop. During the height of the summer season, be sure to make dinner reservations as soon as you arrive, since Spinnaker's is very popular.

Staying There

The American Hotel (516-725-3535) is a nineteenth-century brick building with white cornices and a simple front porch that looks out on Main Street. The first floor features a charming but expensive restaurant, with indoor and outdoor seating. Guest rooms are tastefully decorated with nineteenth-century furnishings.

* * *

If you spend the night in Sag Harbor, you can take in a movie on Main Street, or reserve tickets in advance to a play at the Bay Street Theatre (516-725-9500). The Bay Street Theatre has been called "a major showcase for new plays" by the *New York Times*. Tickets cost you half the price of those on Broadway.

Woodstock, NY

. . . echoes of the 1960s

DAY OR WEEKEND TRIP

Getting There

Adirondack Trailways buses (800-858-8555) leave from Port Authority and go directly to the Village Green in Woodstock. The trip takes approximately two and a half hours.

Being There: Then and Now

As the bus glides into the village of Woodstock, a handsome sign announces "Welcome to Woodstock—Colony of the Arts." Woodstock gained its reputation as a haven for individualism in 1845, when a gathering of Woodstockers disguised themselves as Indians and tarred and feathered the local rent collector.

An art colony called the Byrdcliffe Crafts Colony was established here in 1902. Between 1910 and 1916 the Woodstock Artists Association and the Maverick Concerts (America's first summer chamber music festival) were conceived by painters and musicians who were captivated by this lovely hamlet, sheltered in the valley of the Overlook and Catskill

Mountain ranges. In the years that followed (even before Woodstock gained world renown for the 1969 music festival), icons of the sixties, such as Bob Dylan and Jimi Hendrix made Woodstock their home.

In the warm months, there are flowers everywhere. And shops with names like Modern Mythology, Stone Peace, and Not Fade Away line the roads.

Seeing and Doing

You can have a wonderful weekend in Woodstock, browsing in boutiques and specialty shops, exploring galleries, and hiking country trails. The Artists Association, on Tinker Street near the village green, has information about current activities.

Just behind the Center for Photography of Woodstock (59 Tinker Street) on the banks of Tannery Brook is Tinker Village, a collection of tiny flower-laden huts. The Village's little shops sell flowers, pottery, and affordable antiques and collectibles. Tinker Street has several shops and galleries, including Third Eye Sights, offering exquisite photographs of sacred sites, and the Ann Leonard Gallery, featuring sculpture, paintings, graphics, and jewelry. During spring and summer, there is a large flea market every Saturday from dawn to dusk at the end of Mill House Road.

You can take a tour of the Tibetan Buddhist Monastery (tours are held at 1:30 on Saturdays and Sundays) located at 352 Meads Mountain, about two miles from the town center. The walk from town is quite scenic and lovely. After your visit to the monastery, consider heading on to Overlook Mountain to do a bit of trailblazing.

Eating There

Bistros, cafes, and cozy restaurants can be found on Tinker Street and Mill Hill Road. The Tinker Street Café cooks up delicious burgers, as well as generous sandwiches, at affordable prices. Blue Stone Country, across the road and "set back a bit" also sells casual fare, and you can lunch in their pebbled outdoor garden. Bread Alone, 22 Mill Road, sells sandwiches on breads fresh from a wood-fired brick oven; you can buy whole loaves too. Joshua's Café, 51 Tinker Street, is famous for its four-star dining.

Staying There

We visited the very affordable Twin Gables, 73 Tinker Street (914-679-9479), about a block from where the bus pulls in. Named for its twin-gabled roofs, this bright yellow clapboard home opened its doors for lodging in the 1930s. The ambiance and furnishings of the nine guest rooms reflect the period. Some rooms have baths and some have bath shares.

The Woodstock Inn, on Mill Stream, 38 Tannery Road (914-679-8211), about two and a half blocks from the bus stop, has the ambiance of a bed-and-breakfast with motel privacy. It has eighteen units, serves a delicious breakfast, and features a classic swimming hole.

* * *

Woodstock is a state of mind, as well as a delicious place to visit—so enjoy!

Bethlehem, PA

... repository of Moravian culture

WEEKEND TRIP

Getting There

The Transbridge bus (800-962-9135) goes from Port Authority to South Bethlehem, and the stop is within walking distance of two lodging accommodations we recommend. To get to the historic district, you'll walk over the righthand side of a bridge that crosses the Lehigh River. It's a ten-minute walk with striking views of the river and the townscape.

Being There: Then and Now

In 1741 bands of Moravians (the oldest Protestant denomination) left their homes in Germany and came to the colonies as missionaries seeking converts in the New World. Settling in the lush area beside the Lehigh River and Monocacy Creek, they brought with them their devotion to industry, culture, art, education, and their abiding belief in the equality of women.

The streets are lined with well-preserved, still-occupied buildings, dating back to the eighteenth and nineteenth centuries. On Main Street, the evening lamplight from Victorian street lamps glows softly upon the brick-and-slate patterned walkways, hitching posts, and stone watering troughs.

Seeing and Doing

As you cross the bridge into the historic district, you see the bell-shaped tower of the Central Moravian Church on the corner of Main and Church Streets. To your right is the fieldstone Single Brethren House, erected in 1748, where single men lived before they married. George Washington made it a hospital during the Revolutionary War. Most of the other old buildings are on Church Street, but make your first stop the Bethlehem Chamber of Commerce at 509 Main Street. There you can purchase a booklet with a self-guided tour about the two city blocks between Broad and Church Streets that spans three centuries. Highlights include the Single Sisters House, built in 1772, the Moravian College, and the five-story log Moravian Museum of Bethlehem, the oldest structure in the district. Also of note is the eighteenth-century industrial area below Main Street alongside Monocacy Creek. Here, a small limestone building constructed in 1762, and now a national historic landmark, housed the first municipal water system in the American colonies. The Kemerer Museum of Decorative Arts, on New Street, has rooms of colonial and Victorian furnishings and the largest collection of Bohemian glassware in the States.

For shopping, Main and Broad Streets have beautiful shops—vast, airy spaces full of exquisite clothing, jewelry, antiques, and remarkable collectibles.

As you can imagine, Bethlehem goes all out for Christmas. The tradition began on Christmas Eve in 1741, when a small group of Moravian settlers celebrated the holiday in the tiny log cabins that were their first homes in this country. Singing and carrying lighted candles, they named their new village Bethlelem. Today, the entire town glows with sparkling trees and candlelit windows, while a ninety-one-foot-high shining "North Star" atop South Mountain, towers over Bethlehem and can be seen for many miles. If you want to visit Bethlehem during the Christmas season, you have to make hotel reservations at least eight months in advance.

Bethlehem is also a lively place to be in summer, especially in August, when the city plays host to the week-long Musik Fest.

Eating There

Since 1760, the Sun Inn (564 Main Street, 610-866-1758) has welcomed such famous guests as Benjamin Franklin, George and Martha Washington, Samuel and John Adams, Ethan Allen, and the Marquis de Lafayette. Restored to its authentic Moravian architectural style, its first floor is now a museum, with costumed guides who recount its rich and colorful history. On the second floor, you can dine in an eighteenth-century atmosphere.

The Moravian Book Shop, on Main Street, which carries books of every age, size, and description and has a gift shop, features a small serve-yourself restaurant. The fare is light gourmet, delicious, and reasonably priced. Ana Mia, on Fourth Street, is a beautiful Italian restaurant in a former home. To get there, walk up New Street along Third.

Staying There

Just a block from the little gray trailer that houses the South Bethlehem bus station is the Comfort Suites Motel (800-228-5150), a clean, contemporary complex of 124 newly decorated suites complete with microwave ovens, refrigerators, and cable TV with free HBO. Rates are reasonable. To get there, turn left from the bus stop and walk half a block to Third Street, turn left again, and the hotel is on the next corner.

For a posh overnight stay (great for sharing with friends) we recommend the Sayre Mansion Inn (610-882-2100), where prices are about $100-$125 a night. You can walk there from the bus station, following the same path as the one to Comfort Suites, then continue up the hill to 250 Wyandotte Street. The walk takes about five minutes, or you can call a cab from the bus station. The inn was once the home of Robert Heysham Sayre, an industrialist who shared it with his wife and eleven children. Sayre Mansion has two enchanting parlor rooms, each with its own cozy fireplace, and nineteen antique-filled guest rooms with private baths and modern amenities.

Bethlehem's historic district has the flavor of a small European town. Being there is like visiting another country. It was one of our most enjoyable excursions.

Travel Notes

Three
to
Four
Hours

Mystic, CT

. . . historic seaport with tall ships and
soaring church spires

WEEKEND TRIP

Getting There

Amtrak trains (800-USA-RAIL) go directly from Grand Central Station to Mystic. It's a three-hour trip through lovely scenery, and the train stops right at the edge of downtown.

Being There: Then and Now

Founded in the seventeenth century, the town of Mystic quickly became a shipbuilding center. Now drawing visitors from all across the country, this small seaport city satisfies a yearning to experience America's nautical past.

At the Mystic Seaport Museum, you can explore four magnificent tall ships, from the crews' quarters below the decks to the huge masts above. The museum's holdings also include hundreds of small boats and a number of historic shops and houses.

Amble through an old-time grocery store, a schoolhouse, and a printer's shop. On display are maritime artifacts including majestic ship figureheads and nautical instruments, as well as toys that kept children happy during long-ago journeys over the sea. Be sure to spend some time in the planetarium, where you can learn about the wonders of celestial navigation.

Seeing and Doing

You need at least an extended weekend to sample all of Mystic's offerings. To reach Main Street, walk over the charming Bascule drawbridge. The downtown area has many historic homes, antique emporiums, boutiques, interesting gift shops, and restaurants. You can take half- and full-day sails on the Charlotte Anne, a completely refurbished schooner built in 1888, from Steamboat Wharf in downtown Mystic in the spring and summer (806-536-0416).

Old Mystic Village, on Cogan Boulevard, is a half-hour walk from downtown. This charming replica of a New England village, complete with white clapboard church, is a shopping complex of stores selling an assortment of goods.

Besides the Seaport Museum there's the Mystic Aquarium, featuring fabulous performances by dolphin, seals, and whales. If you're visiting from April to October, a trolley can transport you from downtown Mystic to the aquarium (as well as to other attractions); at other times of year you need to take a taxi since the trolley doesn't run and it's at least a four-mile hike.

For more information and a comprehensive walking tour of the village's historic sites, call the Mystic Tourist Information Center (860-536-1641).

Eating There

There are many pubs, cafes, and fine restaurants on Main Street that you're sure to find a few that will especially appeal to you. Most feature seafood specialties, with an abundant selection of lobster, shrimp, and crabmeat entrées and appetizers. We enjoyed a bowl of clam chowder and a glass of fine merlot at Giaco's Ships Lantern Restaurant on Main Street during a brisk November afternoon. You may want to have a slice at Mystic Pizza of movie fame. The pizza is excellent, even if Julia Roberts doesn't serve you. At The Whaler's Inn, on South Main, you can dine outdoors under a huge open tent in spring and summer.

Staying There

Mystic has many overnight lodging options. Call the Chamber of Commerce (860-572-9578) for a complete list. We stayed at The Whaler's Inn, 20 East Main Street (800-243-2588) because of its charm and proximity to the historic downtown area and the railroad station. A three-story clapboard "home," its lobby resembles a cozy parlor room, and its guest rooms are immaculate and pleasantly furnished with large, comfortable beds. Ask about weekend packages.

* * *

You might also like to spend a couple of hours in Stonington, an old whaling village, just a short cab ride away. Rows of Victorian homes and sea captain's houses line the winding narrow streets. It is hard to imagine that this serene little whitewashed town has changed at all since the seventeenth century, when it lured luminaries such as James Whistler, Stephen Vincent Benét, and Edgar Allan Poe.

Baltimore, MD

. . . glorious Inner Harbor; Fells Point—
a delightful fishing village

WEEKEND TRIP; KID-FRIENDLY

Getting There

Amtrak trains (800-USA-RAIL) go directly to Baltimore from Penn Station. The ride takes about three and a half hours. Greyhound (800-231-2222) and Trailways buses (800-343-9999) depart for Baltimore from Port Authority. Although the ride takes about an hour longer than the train, it costs less. Whichever option you choose, you need to take a taxi from the station in Baltimore to your hotel (there are always plenty waiting at both stations).

Being There: Then and Now

Baltimore is a city of diverse ethnic neighborhoods. In the mid-1900s, many immigrants who passed through Baltimore stayed and found work in the canneries and on the railroads. They lived in Baltimore's well-known row houses, with their characteristic scrubbed-white marble steps, which were built at low cost so that workers could own their own homes. From these humble beginnings, Baltimore has become a town with sophisticated neighborhoods. Writer Anne Tyler, filmmaker Barry Levinson, and jazz greats Billie Holiday and Eubie Blake have all made their homes in Baltimore.

Seeing and Doing

Baltimore has much to offer visitors, and you'll want to return to see and do more. Start with two of our favorite destinations—the exciting Inner Harbor and the delightful historic district of Fells Point.

The Inner Harbor has come a long way since the British shelled its Ft. McHenry during the War of 1812 and inspired Francis Scott Key to write the *Star-Spangled Banner*. Today this area has been renovated into a magnificent public promenade and waterfront plaza. Luxurious hotels, glass-enclosed restaurants, and shops surround the promenade, and it's the setting for festivals all summer long. Two great attractions for children, The Museum of Science and the National Aquarium (with the biggest shark tank in America), anchor the Inner Harbor. The harbor bustles with paddleboats, water taxis, cruise boats, and a tall ship. By the way, the Inner Harbor is within easy walking distance of Baltimore's gorgeous new retro baseball stadium.

After enjoying the activities on the Inner Harbor, board a bright red trolley on Light Street and travel up elegant Charles Street getting off and on at different locations as you please. This hilly street is lined with art galleries and boutiques leading to Mt. Vernon Square, a park ringed by splendid mansions.

Water taxis go back and forth between Fells Point and

the Inner Harbor. A five-minute ride costs about $2.00, but you can also take a trolley. Fells Point is a charming waterfront community of quaint row houses along cobblestone streets. It is also home to many restaurants, art galleries, antique shops, boutiques, collectible emporiums, and bookstores, as well as the occasional tin-ceilinged bar once patronized by shipbuilders, seamen, and merchants during the days when clipper ships and schooners were built in the local shipyards.

Walk along beautiful Ann Street and note the one-of-a-kind decorative screen doors on many of the homes. The scenic paintings on the doors prevent passersby from seeing in, while the screens permit the cool river breezes to circulate inside—a big help to the sweltering inhabitants before the days of fans and air conditioners.

Eating There

Fells Point restaurants include charming bistros, cafes, and century-old taverns. The seafood featured in many restaurants is caught from Maryland's famous Chesapeake Bay. One of the best-known seafood spots is Bertha's, at 734 South Broadway (410-327-5795), a cozy tavern that boasts the town's largest variety of dishes prepared with mussels. You can indulge in mussels with anchovy, tomato, and garlic butter; with spinach, tarragon, and garlic sauce; or with sour cream and scallions. Another well-known seafood spot is Francie's Restaurant & Row Bar, 1629 Thomas Street, with its wide decks stretching along the water. The Wharf Rat Bar, 801 South Ann Street (401-276-9034), is an active, colorful hangout, featuring twenty-seven varieties of beer on tap.

You can get a great cup of coffee at the Daily Grind Coffee House, 1726 Thames Street (410-558-0399), in a low-lit, spacious setting decorated with local art.

The Inner Harbor has a wide variety of restaurants, as well as a huge indoor food court, featuring many different cuisines plus fresh crabs, oysters, and clams at Phillips, Baltimore's most famous seafood restaurant.

Staying There

Fells Point: Ann Street Bed and Breakfast, at 804 South Ann Street (410-342-5883), is comprised of a pair of eighteenth-century restored colonial houses complete with fireplaces, private baths, colonial pine furnishings, and a lovely garden where breakfast is served. The Inn at Henderson's Wharf, 1200 Fell Street (410-522-7777 or 800-522-2088), offers 38 rooms and was formerly a nineteenth-century tobacco warehouse. Situated right on the waterfront, this gracious bed and breakfast has its own dock where a water taxi can pick you up and later return you to your front door. The rooms, decorated in English country style, look out on a lush garden with splashing fountains. Admiral Fell Inn, 888 South Broadway (410-522-7377), is located near the water's edge and offers rooms with Federal Period furnishings.

Inner Harbor: High-rise hotels, such as the Marriott, Sheraton, and Hyatt surround the Inner Harbor. A smaller, elegant, European-style hotel, the Harbor Court, 550 Light Street (800-824-0076), is famous for its library, which contains books from all over the world.

Kripalu Center, Lenox

MASSACHUSETTS

. . . health and yoga retreat in a breathtaking setting

WEEKEND TRIP

Getting There

Bonanza buses (800-556-3815) leave Port Authority for
Lenox, Massachusetts, three times a day. The bus ride takes
just under four hours. Call a taxi (Alstons, 637-3676) from
the pay phone at the bus stop to take you the two miles to
Kripalu. If you prefer, taxi arrangements can be made in
advance by calling 800-286-3674.

Being There: Then and Now

A former Jesuit seminary on a 300-acre wooded site in the
Berkshire Mountains, laid out by Frederick Law Olmsted
and adjacent to Tanglewood, this sprawling four-story brick
building was built in 1957. From the road you see a simple, if
not Spartan, hilltop red-brick structure; but from inside looking out of any window (and they are vast in size and number) are magnificent scenescapes of gardens and lakefront,

and ranges of green-carpeted mountains spilling up into endless sky.

In this exquisite natural setting, Kripalu is a sanctuary where you can relax your body, calm your mind, and strengthen yourself inside and outside.

Seeing and Doing

The activities at Kripalu are designed to bring you to new levels of vibrant health, peace of mind, and spiritual attunement. Skilled instructors will guide you in yoga, meditation, relaxation, moving on (releasing past; embracing new possibilities), transforming stress, and healing. Classes and workshops also include African drumming, mask-making, dreamwork, painting, writing, dancing, singing, and chanting.

You can attend daily workshops of many types; just read or reflect in the deep-cushioned couches and chairs; write at the small wicker desks that furnish the tree-filled Sunroom (open 24 hours); walk on the trails; relax in the whirlpools and saunas, or browse in the Kripalu Shop among a wide selection of books, videotapes, audiotapes, bodycare items, natural-fiber clothing, handcrafted jewelry, crystals, candles, and delicious snacks.

The following events take place daily and participation is welcome, but not required: yoga and meditation at 6 A.M., yoga posture and breathing workshops and danskinetics (rhythms and movements based on yoga) at noon, meditation in the chapel at 5 P.M., and satsanga (coming together to connect with others, support, celebrate, and share) and other evening events at 7:30 P.M.

Eating There

Meals are served cafeteria style three times a day in a large, bright country dining hall, where you eat at long wooden tables. You can chat with other guests at lunch and dinner, but breakfast is designated as a silent meal to provide tranquil time to get ready for the day's activities.

The delectable food is strictly vegetarian: Meals are rich in protein and fiber and moderately low in fats and sweeteners—fresh vegetables and homebaked breads abound. The evening meal might be luscious lasagna (with or without cheese), a tasty curry, hearty squash-and-potato stew, or one of a variety of Mexican-style combinations. You can eat to your heart's content and even learn to love tofu—we did.

Staying There

Accommodations range from dormitory rooms with clean, comfortable bunk beds to more spacious rooms furnished in white wicker with queen-size and twin beds to small, simple rooms with twin beds. There are several large, immaculate bathrooms to share on every floor. Only a few rooms have private baths.

*   *   *

Open throughout the year, Kripalu is a place for all seasons. In the fall, the foliage is magnificent, and in summer you can swim and sun by the lake.

For current information, program schedule, and catalog, call 800-741-7353. Rates include workshops, program activities, meals, and accommodations.

Lenox, MA

. . . cultural center in the foothills
of the Berkshire Mountains

WEEKEND TRIP

Getting There

Bonanza buses (800-556-3815) leave from Port Authority for Lenox three times a day, arriving just across the road from Lenox Town Hall. The nearly four-hour trip from Manhattan takes you through hilly farmland, low stone walls, and covered bridges along one of the most scenic routes in America—Connecticut's Route 7. The bus makes stops in the picturesque New England villages of Kent, Sheffield, Great Barrington, and Stockbridge.

Being There: Then and Now

Dubbed as the "inland Newport," Lenox served as a retreat and summer home for the wealthy and for many literary greats during the mid-nineteenth century. A community of extravagant summer "cottages" sprang up, along with a multitude of cultural activities. Longfellow, Melville,

Hawthorne, Henry Adams, and Edith Wharton gathered here to write. All described the beauty of Lenox, its hilly terrain, and the spectacular Berkshire Mountains.

Today, Lenox is the site of a variety of cultural pursuits, particularly during mild weather. It is the summer home of the Boston Symphony Orchestra at Tanglewood and of Jacob's Pillow, which features some of the finest dance in the country. In spring and fall the scenery is gorgeous, and in winter, several nearby ski slopes are popular destinations.

Seeing and Doing

Once the crowds for the music and dance festivals have retreated, a serenity fills the air and there is still enough activity to engage a curious traveler. Take your pick from chamber music concerts, high teas, cross-country skiing, birdwatching treks, lolling about in an old-fashioned inn, reading under the green banker's lamps at the famous Lenox Library, or browsing through the boutiques and collectibles shops that line Church and Walker Streets. Concepts of Art, 65 Church Street (413-637-4845), carries a unique line of Judaica, including books, paintings, sculptures, jewelry, and other objets d'art.

Although some inns are closed during the off-season (winter and early spring), room rates are lower at these times. Lenox is a town of antiques shops, clothing stores, galleries, churches, historic buildings, and wooded parks. You can rent a bike, a canoe, in-line skates, snowshoes, skis, tennis racquets, and roller blades at the Sport Store on Main Street (413-637-3353)—they have information on bicycle routes, hiking trails, and guided outdoor tours. At the Chamber of

Commerce, also on Main Street, pick up a copy of *Walking Through Lenox History.*

Housed in a landmark building with domed ceilings and marble walls, the Lenox Library on Main Street is open all week long and on weekends till 7 P.M. High-backed wing chairs are clustered about a fireplace in a reading room that features a wide selection of old books and magazines, as well as contemporary titles. Be sure to stop by—it is the most beautiful library we have ever seen.

You can walk or bicycle over to the Mount, where Edith Wharton wrote some of her most important novels (Ethan Frome was based on a sledding accident that took place in Lenox at the bottom of Court House Hill). Perched on a knoll of landscaped gardens that Wharton created and called her "outdoor rooms," this grand house was designed by the writer in 1901. To reach the Mount, walk down Kimble Street to where it meets route 7A.

Eating There

Lenox has a variety of restaurants, some sophisticated and others simple and casual. The Church Street Cafe (65 Church) located in a white clapboard house, specializes in Italian cuisine. We had an assortment of appetizers, along with a carafe of merlot and a basket of home-baked bread. The Roseborough Grill (71 Church) is a friendly country cafe with indoor and outdoor tables, serving New England and continental menus. The Church Street Deli (37 Church) features hot sandwiches, chili, and French onion soup as well as bagels with cream cheese and lox.

Staying There

We stayed at the Gables Inn at 81 Walker Street (413-637-3416). Just a few steps from the bus stop, it's a beautifully restored hundred-year-old Queen Anne Berkshire "cottage" that was the home of Edith Wharton's mother-in-law. Wharton spent two years writing short stories in its library. A stay here is a visit to the Gilded Age: You'll find damask wallpaper, thick Oriental rugs, shaded Victorian lamps, a collection of porcelain dolls, wood-burning fireplaces, and plush curved-back couches upholstered with vivid floral brocades. Bookshelves line the parlor walls, and there's always an open bottle of port and crystal glasses, so help yourself. Many guest rooms have canopied four poster beds and fireplaces; most have private baths. There are no televisions or telephones in the rooms, although there is a large TV in the main parlor.

The Gables serves a full breakfast of pancakes or waffles, eggs, juice, homebaked muffins, melon, and tea or coffee in the lavish dining room. Leaded floor-to-ceiling windows look out over the pool and tennis courts. Classical music plays softly in the background.

We also visited the Gateway's Inn, a few doors past the Gables, at 51 Walker Street (413-637-2532). Built in 1912 as a summer home for Harley Procter of Procter & Gamble, some say the inn's design is reminiscent of a bar of Ivory Soap. The rooms have antique furnishings and private baths, and some have working fireplaces. During his Tanglewood performances, Arthur Fiedler, the late conductor of the Boston Pops, spent many summers in the spacious suite that now bears his name. For more than fourteen years, the inn's restaurant has received Mobil's 4-Star rating—only four other New England restaurants can lay claim to this honor.

Built in 1771, the Village Inn, just around the corner at 16 Church Street (413-637-0020), has thirty-two guest rooms furnished with country antiques; some with working fireplaces and canopy beds. All have private baths. Its restaurant serves breakfast, traditional afternoon English tea, and candlelit dinners in summer and fall. The downstairs Tavern features English ales, draught beer, and a light menu.

Stockbridge, MA

... welcome to Norman Rockwell country

WEEKEND TRIP

Getting There

Bonanza buses (800-556-3815) out of Port Authority stop right in front of the Red Lion Inn. Although the ride takes four hours, the scenery (especially on Route 7, which begins in Connecticut) is spectacular, the bus is air conditioned, and the seats are comfortable.

Being There: Then and Now

In the mid-1800s the Housatonic Railway came through Stockbridge, and wealthy families, discovering the beauty of the area, built lavish summer "cottages," there and in nearby Lenox. A literary colony formed, followed by theater, classical music, and dance programs that have continued up to today and now draw people to the Berkshires from all over the United States.

Many visitors stay at the Red Lion Inn. At one time, the site was the home of the Mahkeenac Indian tribe. Upon their departure, Colonialist Silas Pepoon established the Red Lion.

By 1773, the Red Lion tavern was a stagecoach stop and the village center for discussing politics. At a major convention held at the tavern on July 6, 1774, colonists resolved to boycott British goods in protest of the five Intolerable Acts which Britain had passed in response to the Boston Tea Party. In 1896, the original Red Lion Inn burned to the ground but was rebuilt and reopened the following year with few changes. Today the Red Lion Inn belongs to the Fitzpatricks, a family dedicated to maintaining its historical majesty.

Staying There

If we were to daydream about the perfect country inn, we couldn't come any closer than the Red Lion (413-298-5545). It's splendid and simple at the same time. Red-carpeted steps lead to a wide veranda, dotted with rockers and wicker chairs. Oak doors are opened for you by uniformed attendants as you step into a lobby of exquisite Victorian charm. Oriental rugs, plump period sofas and chairs all reflect the grandeur of the times. A brass "birdcage" elevator takes you to your floor, where long carpeted corridors lead to simply furnished rooms. The hotel has added some modern amenities and there is a library on the third floor, a courtyard dining area, and a swimming pool (some modern amenities do nothing to detract from the nineteenth-century atmosphere).

Call the Red Lion for room rates and reservations. Some small rooms, with bathrooms down the hall, go for less than $100.00 a night.

Seeing and Doing

When you've done enough rocking on the old front porch, and inhaled enough fresh mountain air, you'll be ready for the wonderful shopping in Stockbridge. The original Yankee Candle makes its home on Main Street, and there are numerous collectibles shops and boutiques all around town.

Just across the street at the tiny Chamber of Commerce, you can pick up literature about Stockbridge and look out on the streetscape that was the setting for Norman Rockwell's famous painting *Main Street Stockbridge at Christmastime* (prints can be bought in many shops around town). Rockwell, whose studio was in the center of town, made Stockbridge his home for the last twenty-five years of his life.

In 1986, the studio was moved to the site of the Rockwell Museum, about two miles away. The museum and studio are set on thirty-six hilly acres overlooking the Housatonic River. At the front desk of the Red Lion you can ask for a little map to show you a simple way to walk there. Biking is also an option.

Down the road from the Rockwell Museum is the Berkshire Botanical Gardens. Founded in 1934, it is one of the oldest horticulture centers in the U.S. The gardens are open from May through October and will treat you to a wonderland of spring and summer blooms.

If you're up for a hike through glacial boulders, walk over to the Ice Glen area—a few blocks from Main Street—at the end of Park Street. Cross the footbridge over the Housatonic River and follow the challenging marked trail up the slopes through an ancient scene of glaciers, where ice crystals can be seen even in summer. The summit of your exploration is Laura's Tower, from which you can see Mt. Everette to the southwest, the Catskills of New York to the west, and Vermont's Green Mountains to the north. The hike can take several hours, so be sure to bring drinks and munchies for the journey.

For a fabulous sidetrip from Stockbridge, we suggest an expedition into Great Barrington, another beautiful New England town with a little more urban flair—it has sophisticated boutiques, antique stores, and sushi bars. To get to Great Barrington, you can take a local bus that stops in front of the Chamber of Commerce (right across the street from the Red Lion). The trip takes about a half an hour and runs every hour. Ask the driver to let you off near Railroad Street.

We loved ambling around the fabulous boutiques and other chic shops on Castle and Railroad Streets. The Yellow Bookshop on Main Street was especially good for browsing. We did not stay overnight in Great Barrington; however, if you want information about lodgings in town, call 800-237-5747.

Eating There

The dining options at the Red Lion Inn include the elegant main dining room, where jackets are required for gentlemen and no blue jeans may be worn at the evening meal; the rustic Widow Bingham's Tavern for intimate and more casual dining; and The Lion's Den, where we enjoyed lighter fare for dinner at lighter prices, along with entertainment. There are several restaurants on Main Street, and we had a delicious lunch in the garden of Teresa's, which was the original "Alice's Restaurant," famous for the movie and song of the same name.

*   *   *

Like the other trips in this three to four hour category, Stockbridge makes a delightful extended weekend or mid-week trip and can be visited any time of year. You need to make plans well in advance, however, if you'd like to visit during the busy summer and fall foliage seasons.

Lancaster, PA

. . . center of Amish life and culture

WEEKEND TRIP

Getting There

Amtrak trains (800-872-7245) leave from Penn Station for Lancaster five times a day and the trip takes three and a half hours. Capital Trailways buses leave from Port Authority (212-564-8484) for Lancaster several times a day and that ride also takes about three and a half hours, however the bus is considerably less expensive than the train. A taxi to the Hotel Brunswick at Chestnut and Queen Streets is only about $3.

Being There: Then and Now

Settled in the early 1700s by Swiss Mennonites, Lancaster County soon became home to a large population of Amish, inspired by William Penn's promise of religious freedom and good farmland.

The Amish call themselves "plain people," and they try to keep their lives as simple as when they first came to this country. No modern devices. No electricity. No motor-driven vehicles. No indoor telephones. Horse and buggies are the only means of travel.

Seeing and Doing

Twisting cobblestone paths lead from the Hotel Brunswick up to Central Market. Dating back to the 1730s, this is the oldest covered market in the nation. It has been splendidly restored with distinctive towers, gas lamps, and red-brick facade. Inside is a bountiful array of homegrown produce from the surrounding farms, as well as jams and jellies, breads and pastries, meats and cheeses, and crafts. We were happy to see the ethnic variety of peddlers and foods, ranging from "low-fat" hams to kosher baked goods, to humus and stuffed grape leaves. The market is open from 6 A.M. to 4:30 P.M. weekdays, until 2 P.M. Saturdays, and closed all day Sunday.

Meandering on brick roads through courtyards and alleyways, you come upon hitching posts still used by Lancaster's Amish for their horses and buggies, and by the city's mounted police. Shops and galleries appear at every turn, selling everything from country crafts and quilts to sophisticated art and sculpture.

Leaving the Central Market area, take a right on King Street and follow King until it intersects with Prince Street. There you'll see the Fulton Opera House, a national historic landmark built in 1852, and currently home to several popular theater companies. Also on Prince is the Angry Young & Poor Punk Record & Clothing Shop, where we saw a poster announcing the coming of "The Creeper," a new shoe from Manchester, England. A few doors down is a bookstore specializing in hard-to-find books. Although it's closed on Sundays, you can browse through outdoor shelves and purchase a book by the honor system, dropping a dollar or two into the mail slot at the bottom of the door. On Queen Street, just past the Brunswick Hotel, is a modern multiplex movie theater.

Country Jaunts

The main reason most travelers come to Lancaster County is to visit the quaint villages and farms nestled in the Amish countryside. Pay special attention to the details of this section, since getting around without a car can be tricky, and, according to the advice of a number of locals, "just can't be done." Well, it *can*. We researched and designed original and (we think) ingenious ways to explore the area without a car.

For a tour of the Amish countryside, you have two options. You can take a city bus, which will drop you off at the Plain & Fancy Farm, on Old Philadelphia Pike, or you can taxi over (about a mile) to Days Inn, next to the train station, and a tour bus will pick you up there. For schedules and cost, call Amish Country Tours at 717-768-8400 before you book your hotel reservations. The two-and-a-half-hour tour originates at the Plain & Fancy Farm and includes a visit to a one-room Amish schoolhouse, a bakery and craft shop, and an Amish home. When the bus returns to the farm, there is a tour of a nine-room farmhouse and a movie about Amish life.

Now, here is the tricky part: How do you get back to the hotel when the tour is over? It's time to pull out your White Horse bus schedule. Notice that there is often quite a time lag between buses, but they do run on a very strict schedule and will be on time. In addition to the designated bus stops, there is a flag policy, and you can wave down the bus as long as you're traveling in the same direction.

If you have time after your tour is over, you can have

lunch at Plain & Fancy in one of the "family-style" restaurants, take a buggy ride, or make your way over to the village of Bird-In-Hand, about a mile and a half down the road. (Most likely, one of your fellow tour-takers will give you a lift—if not, it's walking distance, so bring along your walking shoes!) Here you'll have time to explore the shops until your bus is scheduled to arrive at the Bird-In-Hand bus stop at Ronks and Old Philadelphia Pike. The bus will deposit you at Duke and Walnut Street, in front of the old courthouse, and about two blocks from the Brunswick.

The next day, now that you've become a savvy Lancaster City bus rider, you can use the same White Horse schedule to get to the town of Intercourse, a mecca of shops, galleries, and crafts. Again, read your schedule carefully and your trip will go smoothly. You take the bus at Duke and Grant, in front of the old courthouse, and ask the driver to let you off at Intercourse at the corner of Old Philadelphia Pike and Newport. The bus back to Lancaster picks you up at the same stop. Note that the schedules for weekday and Saturday buses are different, and that on Sundays buses do not run to Intercourse and shops are closed.

Another alternative—if you're feeling lazy or luxuriant and don't want to bus it is to call Yellow Cab from Intercourse and have them deliver you right to the hotel door (expect a $22 fare). (Yellow Cab can also pick you up from Lancaster and take you to Intercourse.)

Intercourse, much more crowded with tourists than Bird-In-Hand, brims with shops selling crafts, flowers, candles, handmade quilts, and Amish souvenirs. Many of the shops are owned and operated by the Amish, and their horses and buggies are parked in front of banks and stores, alongside tourist busses and cars. This is the town where the Amish take care of business transactions, and it's always bustling.

Seated at a table next to a Mennonite couple with two perfectly behaved young children, we ate at the Intercourse Village Restaurant (in the Best Western Motel) served by young women in black pinafores and organdy caps.

If you are in Lancaster on a Sunday and want to find out about local history, you can join the one-and-a-half-hour walking tour sponsored by the Chamber of Commerce that leaves at 1:30 P.M. from South Queens Street. Alternatively, you can take a swim in the indoor pool at the Brunswick; and, there's always the fabulous brunch at the Market Fare Restaurant.

Eating There

We started off at House of Pizza, just across Chestnut Street from the Brunswick, which serves not only homemade pizza but a full spectrum of pasta and seafood. The Lancaster Dispensing Company at Market and Orange Streets, in the historic square, is a lively Victorian pub that serves more than fifty varieties of beer from around the world. It offers a selection of hearty soups, sandwiches, and meat and vegetable dishes to a young crowd. There's a happy hour every weekday evening at 5 P.M.—drinks for a dollar along with complimentary hot hors d'oeuvres. Wednesday through Saturday evenings, musicians perform a repertoire ranging from folk and country to rhythm and blues. Just across the road at the corner of Grant and Market is the spacious Market Fare Restaurant where on a late Sunday morning we had a sumptuous, prix-fixe, all-you-can-eat smorgasbord including caviar, mussels, strawberries, cold shrimp, and pecan pies. The inviting Palace on Prince, at Prince and Orange Streets, serves breakfast, lunch, and dinner at reasonable prices.

Staying There

We suggest staying at the Hotel Brunswick (800-233-0182) because of its proximity to the city's historic landmarks, bus station and train terminal (a taxi ride to the hotel from the bus or train is only $3.00—call Yellow Taxi at 397-8100)

A modern hotel with a large comfortable lobby and clean airy rooms, the Brunswick has an indoor pool, a restaurant with a wood-burning fireplace, and a downstairs nightclub called the Library, which features Friday night happy hours, live music and dancing, and a once-a-month "hog roast," compliments of the house.

When you register, be sure to ask the desk clerk for a city bus schedule to White Horse—you may need it for your later adventures. You can also pick a schedule up at the corner of Queen and Chestnut Street at the Rose Transit Company, just a block from the hotel.

Be sure to look at one of the free local newspapers in the lobby to find discount coupons for restaurants and events, or to help you locate activities such as horse-and-buggy rides through the countryside, sit-down dinners with an Amish family, and a morning at a working Amish farm.

Index of Destinations

Index by State

Acknowledgements

We dedicate this book to all those "land-locked" New York City dwellers who heave a sigh at the end of summer, after their two or four-week vacations have ended, plunging into yet another year of unbroken daily grind in the city, who dream and scheme about places to go for their next summer vacation, never realizing that every weekend in the year can be heavenly.

We would like to thank . . .

* the Innkeepers and Hotel Mangers of lodgings described in this book, all of whom generously gave their time to introduce us to the aspects of their establishments which would best serve patrons without a car—recommending nearby eateries and providing us with descriptions of the backgrounds and foregrounds of their surrounding areas, telling us where to go, what to see, and how to get there on foot or by local bus

* the memory of Charles Kuralt, whose chronicle of his journeys to rediscover America by exploring its towns and villages and talking to its people inspired us to continue chronicling the many pertinent details of each journey when our energies flagged

* Cynthia Nichols Mead, for recommending special destinations and accompanying us on several of our journeys

* Beatrice Levy, Sue's mother, and Bernie Platt, Gena's dad, for their continued enthusiasm, ideas, and support

* Marge Halpern for feeding, watering, and loving Jake while Gena "weekended"
* Michael Mannion for his determined encouragement to put this project on paper
* Eric Clemett for his patience and cooperation
* Nicole Vandestienne for her research and exploration of upstate lodgings
* Arlene Hoffman, Adam Tyler, Renee and Laura Franklin for their generous technical assistance on the computer
* Ed McCoyd and the Authors Guide for guidance on how to read a contract
* Paul Filencia, Jennifer Vandestienne and Ed Platt for being there to listen to our travel tales before they were written down
* Tim Haft, Margaret Wolf, Kathy Goldman and Melisa Coburn for their work on our manuscript
* Leah Lococo for her beautiful design and
* Helene Silver at City & Company for her enthusiasm and masterful coordination.

About the Authors

Susan Clemett and Gena Vandestienne met in Greenwich Village on a park bench in Abingdon Square while their toddlers played in a sandbox. When their children became teenagers, these moms went back to school.

Susan received Masters degrees in Education and Counseling. She has been a teacher and a counselor for inner-city youth in New York public schools for many years. Gena received a Masters degree from New York University in Health and Sexuality and has been published in numerous magazines and professional journals.

Heavenly Weekends was born out of their devotion to New York City and all it provides, and their desire to venture beyond its boundaries easily and affordably—always knowing that it is there to come home to.

About the Illustrator

Molly O'Gorman is an illustrator who lives with her two children, Clara and Ted, their dog Duchess, and Trixie the cat, in Rhinebeck, New York. She is represented in the big city by Artworks Illustration.

Travel Notes

Travel Notes

Travel Notes

Other titles from City and Company

Beauty, The Little Black Book for New York Glamour Girls	$12.95
The Big Cup, A Guide to New York's Coffee Culture	$12.95
Brooklyn Eats	$12.00
City Baby	$15.95
City Wedding	$18.00
CityTripping	$15.95
Cool Parents Guide to All of New York	$12.95
Erotic New York	$12.95
Good & Cheap Ethnic Eats in New York City	$16.00
How To Meet a Mensch in New York	$12.95
Ken Druse's New York City Gardener	$15.00
The New York Book of Dance	$14.00
The New York Book of Music	$15.00
The New York Book of Tea, 2nd Edition	$16.00
New York Chocolate Lover's Guide	$16.00
Psychic New York	$13.00
Shop NY/Downtownstyle	$15.95
Shop NY/Jewelry	$15.95
Sports New York	$14.95
Touring Historic Harlem	$14.95
Touring the Flatiron District	$12.00
Touring the Upper East Side	$9.95
A Year in New York	$20.00

New York's 50 Best Places to Find Peace & Quiet $12.00

New York's 50 Best Places to Eat Southern $12.00

New York's 50 Best Places to Take Children $12.00

New York's 50 Best Secret Architectural Treasures $9.95

New York's 50 Best Skyscrapers $12.00

New York's 50 Best Wonderful Little Hotels $12.00

New York's 50 Best Wonderful Things to
    Do During the Holiday Season $12.00

New York's 50 Hottest Nightspots $10.95

You can find all these books
at your local bookstore,
or write to:
City & Company
22 West 23rd Street
New York, NY 10010
212-366-1988
212-242-0415/fax
cityco@bway.net/email